100 LITERACY ASSESSMENT LESSONS

TERMS AND CONDITIONS

IMPORTANT – PERMITTED USE AND WARNINGS – READ CAREFULLY BEFORE USING

Licence

YEAR 1

Scottish Primary 2

Minimum specification:
- PC or Mac with a CD-ROM drive and 512 Mb RAM (recommended)
- Windows 2000 or above/Mac OSX version 10.4 or above
- Recommended minimum processor speed: 1 GHz

For all technical support queries, please phone Scholastic Customer Services on 0845 603 9091.

Gillian Howell

CREDITS

Author
Gillian Howell

Development Editor
Fabia Lewis

Editor
Mike Ward

Series Designers
Joy Monkhouse and
Melissa Leeke

Designers
Andrea Lewis, Allison Parry
and Quadrum Ltd

Illustrations
Anna Godwin/The Illustrator
Agency (unless otherwise
credited)

CD-ROM development
CD-ROM developed in
association with Vivid
Interactive

Text © 2010, Gillian Howell
© 2010, Scholastic Ltd

Designed using Adobe
InDesign

Published by Scholastic Ltd
Book End
Range Road
Witney
Oxfordshire OX29 0YD

Visit our website at
www.scholastic.co.uk

Printed by Bell and Bain Ltd

123456789 0123456789

ACKNOWLEDGEMENTS

The publishers gratefully acknowledge permission to reproduce the following copyright material: **Paul Cookson** for the use of 'These are the hands' by Paul Cookson from *The Works 6* chosen by Pie Corbett © 2007, Paul Cookson (2007, Macmillan). **Peter Dixon** for the use of 'Moving Away' by Peter Dixon from *The Penguin in the Fridge and other cool poems* by Peter Dixon © 2001, Peter Dixon (2001, Macmillan). **Eddison Pearson** for the use of 'Last Lick' by Valerie Bloom from *The Works: Key Stage 1* chosen by Pie Corbett © 2006, Valerie Bloom (2006, Macmillan). **David Harmer** for the use of 'The Really Rocking Rocket Trip' by David Harmer from *The Works: Key Stage 1* chosen by Pie Corbett © 2006, David Harmer (2006, Macmillan). **Emily Hearn** for the use of 'My friend' by Emily Hearn from *The Works: Key Stage 1* chosen by Pie Corbett © 2006, Emily Hearn (2006, Macmillan). **Macmillan Children's Books** for the use of text from *The Gruffalo* by Julia Donaldson text © 1999, Julia Donaldson. **Celia Warren** for the use of 'Lion' from *Hippo Book of Magic Poems* chosen by Jennifer Curry © 1997, Celia Warren (1997, Scholastic).

Every effort has been made to trace copyright holders for the works reproduced in this book, and the publishers apologise for any inadvertent omissions.

British Library Cataloguing-in-Publication Data
A catalogue record for this book is available from the British Library.
ISBN 978-1407-10189-7
The right of Gillian Howell to be identified as the author of this work has been asserted by her in accordance with the Copyright, Designs and Patents Act 1988.

Contents

Introduction 4–7

Periodic assessment 8–9

Narrative 10
Unit 1 10–25
Unit 2 26–41
Unit 3 42–57
Unit 4 58–73

Non-fiction 74
Unit 1 74–83
Unit 2 84–91
Unit 3 92–101
Unit 4 102–113
Unit 5 114–129

Poetry 130
Unit 1 130–145
Unit 2 146–159
Unit 3 160–173

Transitional assessment 174–175

100 Literacy Assessment Lessons: Year 1

'Assessment' refers to all those activities undertaken by teachers, and by their students in assessing themselves, which provide information to be used as feedback to modify the teaching and learning activities in which they are engaged.'

from Black and William *Inside the Black Box*

About the series

100 Literacy Assessment Lessons is a response to the Assessment for Learning strategy (AfL) and Assessing Pupils' Progress (APP) and contains all new, stand-alone material. The lessons mirror the guidelines and viewpoints of the revised approach to assessment. The CD-ROMs provide appropriate and exciting texts and a variety of assessment activities from photocopiable pages for individual, whole-class or group work to stimulating interactive activities. Together, the books and CD-ROMs will be an invaluable resource to help you understand and implement the revised approach to assessment.

About assessment

The key points of the revised approach to assessment are as follows:
- Assessments are accurate and linked to National Curriculum levels;
- Assessments are targeted, with assessment focuses used as the guiding criteria;
- Assessments are reliable and based on a range of evidence;
- Assessments are useful and appropriate: day to day, periodic or transitional.

What are assessment focuses (AFs)?

Assessment focuses (AFs) are tools for assessment that sit between the National Curriculum programmes of study and level descriptions. The AFs provide more detailed criteria against which children's standards of attainment can be assessed and judged.

Type of assessment	Purpose	Strategies
Day to day	Ongoing and formative: encourages reflection and informs the next steps in teaching and learning.	Objectives, outcomes and success criteria are made explicit and are shared with children; observations are used to gather evidence; peer assessment and self-assessment help to develop children as responsible learners.
Periodic	Provides a periodic view of children's progress and diagnostic information linked to national standards.	Progress and attainment are reviewed regularly (half-termly or termly) against APP criteria; strengths and gaps in learning are identified to inform future planning.
Transitional	Brings together evidence, including tests, at points of transition (eg level to level or year to year); provides a formal overview of children's attainment set within the framework of national standards.	Use of formal tasks and tests; external validation and reporting.

For a complete list of strategies for day-to-day assessment and further information about periodic and transitional assessment, visit the National Strategies website (**http://nationalstrategies.standards.dcsf.gov.uk**).

About the book
Reflecting the structure of the renewed Primary Framework for Literacy (2006), the book is divided into three Blocks: Narrative, Non-fiction and Poetry. Each Block is further divided into Units, and the Units are split into Phases. The Phases are divided into a number of day-to-day assessment activities. These assessment activities, based on learning outcomes, are designed to fit easily into your existing planning.

Units
Each Unit covers a different text-type or genre and, because of this, each Unit has its own introduction containing the following:
Literacy objectives: All objectives for the Unit are listed under their strand names.
Key aspects of learning: Aspects of learning that the Unit covers are identified from the renewed Primary National Strategy (PNS) Framework.
Assessment focuses (AFs): The main assessment focuses that are addressed during the Unit are listed from APP.
Speaking and listening: Assessment areas you should look out for are linked to the Speaking and listening strand objectives.
Resources: Lists all of the resources required for the activities in each Phase.
Planning grids: There are two grids per Unit to provide an overview of the Unit and to suggest how you can build assessment opportunities into your medium-term planning. The grids show Phases, learning outcomes, a summary of lessons, assessment opportunities and potential evidence, levelled statements of the assessment focuses (AFs), and success criteria matched to the learning outcomes in the form of 'I can...' statements.

Assessment activities
Each assessment activity follows the same format:
Learning outcomes: These are relevant to individual activities or a set of activities that share objectives.
Success criteria: These are child-friendly 'I can...' statements for children or teachers to refer to during or following the activity.
Setting the context: This section provides guidance on what the task is and details the children's expected prior learning. The context for the task may also be explained: group, paired or individual work. Where adult support is required, this is also described.
Assessment opportunity: This section highlights what to assess, how to find out what children know, and what questions to ask.
Assessment evidence: This section suggests what to look for during an activity in relation to specific assessment focuses (AFs).
Next steps: This section is divided into support and extension. It provides ideas to enable children to revisit an objective or learning outcome, and gives feedback or targets to move children forward, consolidate or extend their learning.
Key aspects of learning: Key aspects of learning are linked to specific activities.

Photocopiable pages
At the end of each Unit is a selection of photocopiable activity pages. The full range of these is provided on the CD-ROM, including levelled versions where appropriate. Photocopiable pages may include self-assessment statements for ticking as well as a 'traffic light' system for colouring (see 'Self-assessment' on page 7 for more information.) Where 'I can...' statements are not included, peer assessment may be suggested within an activity.

Transitional assessment
Also included on the CD-ROM are some SATs-style formal single-level assessments. More information about these can be found on page 7, and a grid detailing their content is provided on page 174.

How to use the materials

The activities in the book provide a balance of whole-class/group/paired/independent learning and teaching, and give the opportunity not only for day-to-day assessment but also for collection of evidence against individual assessment focuses (AFs) for periodic review. Each activity can be slotted into a lesson where appropriate and may involve discussion work, written responses, use of photocopiable pages or interactive activities.

Two periodic assessment activities are provided at the end of each Unit – one for reading and one for writing. The focus of each of these activities is usually a photocopiable page that assesses children on the learning outcomes covered during the Unit and provides further evidence against the assessment focuses. You can also use these periodic assessments to help you to make level judgements that match to the Reading and Writing Attainment Targets (ATs).

Making a level judgement

Assessment involves making a level judgement against national standards at regular intervals. The following steps will support you in adopting a strategic approach to the marking and levelling needed for assessment.

Step one: Consider evidence
● Use a range of appropriate evidence to make a level judgement, for example, written or oral;
● Remember that it is quality not quantity that matters;
● Keep examples of children's work that will provide significant evidence.

Step two: Review the evidence
● Take a broader view of a child's achievement across the whole subject and over time;
● Create a visual picture of strengths and learning gaps by highlighting criteria a child has met across a range of evidence;
● Collaborate with colleagues and agree what constitutes success for the various assessment criteria.

Step three: Make a judgement
● Consult the English Assessment Guidelines (see National Standards website: **http://nationalstrategies.standards.dcsf.gov.uk** and look at exemplar material provided in the Standards files;
● Arrive at an overall subject level judgement;
● Think about what the child demonstrates:
  – How much of the level;
  – How consistently;
  – How independently;
  – In what range of contexts.
● Finally, fine-tune your levelling to 'high', 'secure' or 'low'.

What's on the CD-ROM?

Each CD-ROM contains a wealth of resources. These include:
● **Photocopiable pages:** levelled where appropriate, including text extracts and activity sheets for day-to-day and periodic assessment.
● **Transitional assessments:** single-level tests for levels 1–3 including mark schemes and instructions.
● **Interactive activities:** for individuals or small groups, with in-built marking to assess specific learning outcomes.
● **Whiteboard tools:** a set of tools (including a pen, highlighter, eraser, notes and reward stickers) that can be used to annotate activity sheets or interactive activities. These tools will work on any interactive whiteboard or conventional screen.
● **Editable planning grids** (in Word format) are available to help teachers integrate the assessment activities into their medium-term and weekly planning.

How to use the CD-ROM

System requirements
Minimum specification:
- PC or Mac with a CD-ROM drive and 512 Mb RAM (recommended)
- Windows 2000 or above/Mac OSX version 10.4 or above
- Recommended minimum processor speed: 1 GHz

Getting started
The *100 Literacy Assessment Lessons* CD-ROM should auto run when inserted into your CD drive. If it does not, browse to your CD drive to view the contents of the CD-ROM and click on the *100 Literacy Assessment Lessons* icon.

From the start-up screen you will find four options: select **Credits** to view a list of acknowledgements. Click on **Register** to register the product in order to receive product updates and special offers. Click on **How to use this CD-ROM** to access support notes for using the CD-ROM. Finally, if you agree to the terms and conditions, select **Start** to move to the main menu.

For all technical support queries, contact Scholastic Customer Services help desk on 0845 6039091.

Navigating the CD-ROM
The CD-ROM allows users to search for resources by Block or Unit, or by assessment focus. Users can also search by assessment type (day to day, periodic or transitional) or by resource type (for example, worksheet, interactive resource, or text extract).

Day-to-day assessments
These should be used to support learning. They can be used during a lesson, when you judge that children are ready for an assessment activity. The materials can also be used weekly or after a unit of work has been completed.

Periodic assessments
These can be used with a group of children rather than with the whole class. This could be at the end of a unit of work (for example, at the end of a half-term or term). Decide who is ready to be assessed using the outcomes of the day-to-day assessment activities and your observations of children's performance.

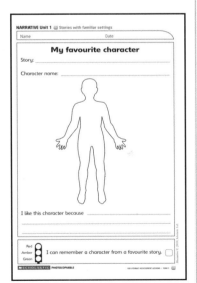

Self-assessment
There is a 'traffic light' system at the bottom of some photocopiable pages that children can shade to show how they feel about the activity: red for 'need help'; orange for 'having some understanding'; green for 'I found this easy!'. (Alternatively, you may wish to utilise these as a teacher marking tool for providing an at-a-glance guide to the child's progress.)

The photocopiable sheets also provide 'I can...' statements with tick boxes, to enable children to self-assess specifically in terms of the relevant learning outcomes/success criteria. A similar system is in place at the end of all the interactive activities, where the children are asked to click on a traffic light, and to type in any comments.

Transitional tests
These single-level tests provide evidence of where, in relation to national standards, children are at a given point in time. There are two Reading and Writing assessments for each level. Each reading assessment consists of a two-part reading comprehension test based on two different text types. Each writing assessment consists of two writing tasks – shorter and longer – that focus on writing for different purposes. All the tasks and tests for levels 2–5 are included on the CD-ROM together with easy-to-follow marking schemes (see pages 174–175 for more information.)

Class PET
A whole-school version of *100 Literacy Assessment Lessons* is available with an expanded range of digital assessment activities, as well as the facility to report, record and track children's work. For further information visit the Class PET website, **www.scholastic.co.uk/classpet**.

Periodic assessment

Unit	AT	Page	Assessment focuses	Learning outcomes
Narrative 1	Reading	20	AF2, AF4	Children can identify the main character and setting in a story using evidence from the illustrations and text.
	Writing	21	AF5, AF7	Children can write three simple sentences to tell a story.
Narrative 2	Reading	38	AF5	Children can recognise language patterns and repeated words and phrases in a text and discuss their effect on a reader.
	Writing	38	AF1	Children can write simple sentences using patterned language, words and phrases taken from familiar stories.
Narrative 3	Reading	53	AF2, AF4	Children can identify the main events in traditional tales, sequencing them in chronological order. Children can say what a playscript is for and can identify some ways in which it differs from a story text.
	Writing	54	AF1, AF8	Children can write a profile of a character using visual and written text. Children can write their own version of a traditional story, using a series of complete sentences organised into chronological order.
Narrative 4	Reading	68	AF2, AF4	Children can predict possible events in a narrative based on their experience of other texts. Children can orally tell an adventure narrative during role play with the events organised sequentially into problem and resolution.
	Writing	69	AF1	Children can compose complete sentences correctly demarcated by capital letters and full stops. Children can write a short story with the events organised sequentially into problem and resolution.
Non-fiction 1	Reading	81	AF4	Children can say what the purposes of lists and labels in the classroom are.
	Writing	81	AF2, AF6	Children write a caption for an object or picture in a complete sentence with a capital letter and full stop.

Unit	AT	Page	Assessment focuses	Learning outcomes
Non-fiction 2	Reading	90	AF4	Children can say whether a text is a fiction or non-fiction text. Children can listen to and follow simple instructions.
	Writing	90	AF2, AF6, AF7	Children can write at least three instructions in a well-rehearsed sequence independently.
Non-fiction 3	Reading	99	AF1	Children can use knowledge of the alphabet to locate words in simple dictionaries.
	Writing	99	AF6	Children can write at least three simple sentences in the past tense and use some time connectives in a recount.
Non-fiction 4	Reading	109	AF4, AF5	Children can say what the key structural features of a simple information text are.
	Writing	109	AF2	Children can write sentences for an information text in an appropriate style.
Non-fiction 5	Reading	125	AF1	Children can sequence a set of events based on their own experience and observations.
	Writing	125	AF3	Children can write a recount using time connectives to sequence events and correctly demarcate sentences.
Poetry 1	Reading	141	AF1, AF5	Children can listen to poems and identify words and phrases that describe what we see, hear, feel (touch), smell and taste.
	Writing	141	AF1	Children can identify detailed sensory responses to direct experience and start to select and write suitable words and phrases to describe these.
Poetry 2	Reading	154	AF5	Children can respond to simple patterned stories, identifying the patterned forms and use of rhymes. Children can hear, read and respond to story written in rhyme.
	Writing	155	AF1	Children can use rhymes and stories as models for their own writing.
Poetry 3	Reading	169	AF4, AF5	Children can identify poetic features and patterns in poems on a common theme.
	Writing	169	AF2	Children can select their favourite poems and give reasons for their choices.

NARRATIVE

UNIT 1 Stories with familiar settings

Literacy objectives

Speak and listen for a wide range of purposes in different contexts

Strand 1 Speaking
- Retell stories, ordering events using story language.
- Tell stories and describe incidents from their own experience in an audible voice.

Strand 2 Listening and responding
- Listen with sustained concentration, building new stores of words in different contexts.

Strand 4 Drama
- Explore familiar themes and characters through improvisation and role play.

Read and write for a range of purposes on paper and on screen

Strand 5 Word recognition: decoding (reading) and encoding (spelling)
- Recognise and use alternative ways of pronouncing the graphemes already taught.
- Identify the constituent parts of two-syllable and three-syllable words to support the application of phonic knowledge and skills.
- Recognise automatically an increasing number of familiar high frequency words.
- Apply phonic knowledge and skills as the prime approach to reading and spelling unfamiliar words that are not completely decodable.
- Read more challenging texts which can be decoded using their acquired phonic knowledge and skills, along with automatic recognition of high frequency words.
- Read and spell phonically decodable two-syllable and three-syllable words.

Strand 6 Word structure and spelling
- Spell new words using phonics as the prime approach.
- Segment sounds into their constituent phonemes in order to spell them correctly.
- Recognise and use alternative ways of spelling the graphemes already taught.
- Use knowledge of common inflections in spelling, such as plurals, -ly, -er.
- Read and spell phonically decodable two-syllable and three-syllable words.

Strand 7 Understanding and interpreting texts
- Identify the main events and characters in stories, and find specific information in simple texts.
- Use syntax and context when reading for meaning.

Strand 8 Engaging with and responding to texts
- Select books for personal reading and give reasons for choices.
- Visualise and comment on events, characters and ideas, making imaginative links to their own experiences.

Strand 9 Creating and shaping texts
- Independently choose what to write about, plan and follow it through.
- Use key features of narrative in their own writing.
- Create short simple texts on paper and screen that combine words with images (and sounds).

Strand 10 Text structure and organisation
- Write chronological and non-chronological texts using simple structures.

Strand 11 Sentence structure and punctuation
- Compose and write simple sentences independently to communicate meaning.

Key aspects of learning

Creative thinking
● Children will apply imaginative ideas to create ideas for drama and story writing based on familiar incidents and settings.

Motivation
● Children will have a clear goal for their independent writing – composing three complete sentences – and will be able to assess their own progress in achieving that goal as they read through what they have written.

Evaluation
● Children will discuss success criteria for their written work, give feedback to others and begin to judge the effectiveness of their own writing.

Communication
● Children will develop their ability to discuss as they work collaboratively in paired, group and whole-class contexts. They will communicate outcomes orally, in writing and through ICT if appropriate.

Assessment focuses

Reading
AF2 *(understand, describe, select or retrieve information, events or ideas from texts and use quotation and reference to text).*
AF6 *(identify and comment on writers' purposes and viewpoints, and the overall effect of the text on the reader).*

Writing
AF1 *(write imaginative, interesting and thoughtful texts).*
AF3 *(organise and present whole texts effectively, sequencing and structuring information, ideas and events).*
AF7 *(select appropriate and effective vocabulary).*

Speaking and listening
Speaking (speak with intonation, clarity and pace).
Listening and responding (listen with sustained concentration).
Drama (improvise and sustain role).

Resources

Phase 1 activities
Photocopiable page, 'My favourite character'
Photocopiable page, 'My favourite story' (versions 1 and 2)
Phase 2 activities
Photocopiable page, 'Telling a story'
Interactive activity, 'Telling a story'
Phase 3 activities
Photocopiable page, 'Make up a story' (versions 1 and 2)
Periodic assessment
Photocopiable page, 'Narrative 1 Reading assessment'

Unit 1 ☐ Stories with familiar settings

Learning outcomes	Assessment opportunity and evidence	Assessment focuses (AFs)	Success criteria
		Level 1	

Phase ① activities pages 15-16

Learning outcomes	Assessment opportunity and evidence	Assessment focuses (AFs) — Level 1	Success criteria
Respond to a story with memories Children can identify the main character and setting in a story using evidence from the illustrations and text.	• Supported activity where children draw and write about a story character from memory. • Whole-class discussion of stories and characters. • Children's oral responses and written responses on the photocopiable page.	**Reading AF2** • Some simple points from familiar texts recalled. • Some pages/sections of interest located. **Writing AF7** • Mostly simple vocabulary. • Communicates meaning through repetition of key words.	• I can remember a favourite story and talk about what happens. • I can remember a character from a favourite story.
Compare stories Children can compare stories and give preferences with reasons.	• Supported activity where children compare three stories and then write and draw about their preferred story. • Group discussion and recall of the three stories. • Children's written responses on the photocopiable page.	**Reading AF6** • Some simple comments about preferences, mostly linked to own experience.	• I can remember a favourite story. • I can compare stories.

Phase ② activities pages 17-18

Learning outcomes	Assessment opportunity and evidence	Assessment focuses (AFs) — Level 1	Success criteria
Telling a story Children can sequence the main events of a story.	• Supported activity where children cut out and sequence three pictures from a story and then write key words or a sentence to caption each picture. • Whole-class discussion and children's oral responses. • Children's sequenced pictures and sentences, and the completed interactive activity.	**Writing AF3** • Some formulaic phrases indicate start/end of text. • Events/ideas sometimes in appropriate order.	• I can retell a story. • I can create a storyboard.
Performing a story Children can re-enact a story, sequencing the main events and using phrases from the text.	• Group activity where children plan and perform a retelling of a familiar story. • Group discussion and performance of the story. • Children's peer evaluations against agreed success criteria.	**Reading AF2** • Some simple points from familiar texts recalled. • Some pages/sections of interest located.	I can perform a story.

Phase ③ activity page 19

Learning outcomes	Assessment opportunity and evidence	Assessment focuses (AFs) — Level 1	Success criteria
Make up a story Children can write three simple sentences to tell a story.	• Independent activity where children complete a story, using images and key words to describe their feelings. • Children's drawings and key words on the completed photocopiable page.	**Writing AF1** • Basic information and ideas conveyed through appropriate word choice. • Some descriptive language.	I can write a story with three sentences.

Unit 1 📖 Stories with familiar settings

NARRATIVE

Learning outcomes	Assessment opportunity and evidence	Assessment focuses (AFs)		Success criteria
		Level 2	Level 3	
Phase ① activities pages 15–16				
Respond to a story with memories Children can identify the main character and setting in a story using evidence from the illustrations and text.	• Group activity where children draw and write about a story character from memory. • Whole-class discussion of stories and characters. • Children's oral responses and written responses on the photocopiable page.	**Reading AF2** • Some specific, straightforward information recalled. • Generally clear idea of where to look for information. **Writing AF7** • Simple, often speech-like vocabulary conveys relevant meanings. • Some adventurous word choices.	**Reading AF2** • Simple, most obvious points identified though there may also be some misunderstanding. • Some comments include quotations from or references to text, but not always relevant. **Writing AF7** • Simple, generally appropriate vocabulary used, limited in range. • Some words selected for effect or occasion.	• I can remember a favourite story and talk about what happens. • I can remember a character from a favourite story.
Compare stories Children can compare stories and give preferences with reasons.	• Independent activity where children compare three stories and then write and draw about their preferred story. • Group discussion and recall of the three stories. • Children's written responses on the photocopiable page.	**Reading AF6** • Some awareness that writers have viewpoints and purposes. • Simple statements about likes and dislikes in reading, sometimes with reasons.	**Reading AF6** • Comments identify main purpose. • Express personal response but with little awareness of writer's viewpoint or effect on reader.	• I can remember a favourite story. • I can compare stories.
Phase ② activities pages 17–18				
Telling a story Children can sequence the main events of a story.	• Independent activity where children cut out and sequence three pictures from a story and then write a sentence to caption each picture. • Whole-class discussion and children's oral responses. • Children's sequenced pictures and sentences.	**Writing AF3** • Some basic sequencing of ideas or material. • Openings and/or closings sometimes signalled.	**Writing AF3** • Some attempt to organise ideas with related points placed next to each other. • Openings and closings usually signalled. • Some attempt to sequence ideas or material logically.	• I can retell a story. • I can create a storyboard.

■ SCHOLASTIC   100 LITERACY ASSESSMENT LESSONS • YEAR 1   **13**

Unit 1 ▢ Stories with familiar settings

Learning outcomes	Assessment opportunity and evidence	Assessment focuses (AFs)		Success criteria
		Level 2	Level 3	
Performing a story Children can re-enact a story, sequencing the main events and using phrases from the text.	• Group activity where children plan and perform a retelling of a familiar story. • Group discussion and performance of the story. • Children's peer evaluations against agreed success criteria.	**Reading AF2** • Some specific, straightforward information recalled. • Generally clear idea of where to look for information.	**Reading AF2** • Simple, most obvious points identified though there may also be some misunderstanding. • Some comments include quotations from or references to text, but not always relevant.	I can perform a story.
Phase ③ activity page 19				
Make up a story Children can write three simple sentences to tell a story.	• Independent activity where children complete a story, using images and sentences to describe their feelings. • Children's drawings and written sentences on the completed photocopiable page.	**Writing AF1** • Mostly relevant ideas and content, sometimes repetitive or sparse. • Some apt word choices create interest. • Brief comments, questions about events or actions suggest viewpoint.	**Writing AF1** • Some appropriate ideas and content included. • Some attempt to elaborate on basic information or events. • Attempt to adopt viewpoint, though often not maintained or inconsistent.	I can write a story with three sentences.

Phase ① Respond to a story with memories

Success criteria
- I can remember a favourite story and talk about what happens.
- I can remember a character from a favourite story.

Setting the context
This assessment should be carried out once the children have had the opportunity to listen to and share in the reading of stories with familiar settings. They should have been introduced to the terms 'character', 'setting' and 'events' and had practice at using these terms when talking about the stories. Ask the children to choose a favourite story from those that have been read recently. Invite them to share, from memory, their favourite character from the story and what they liked about this particular character. Explain that they are going to draw and write about their favourite character using the photocopiable page 'My favourite character'.

Assessment opportunity
Support the children working at level 1 by asking them questions to help them recall details about their favourite character. Children working at levels 2-3 can complete the task in small, independent groups. When the children have completed their pictures, and before they write about their character, invite them to share their descriptions verbally with a talk partner. Encourage them to think about their choice of words. Can they think of any other words that might be better when describing their character?

Assessment evidence
At level 1, the children will use single-word captions or very basic sentences such as 'Funny' or 'He is funny'. At levels 2-3, the children might write a complete sentence using their own vocabulary, including more than one feature. Use the notes made in discussion with the children and the completed photocopiable pages to provide evidence against Reading AF2 and Writing AF7.

Next steps
Support: For children who found it difficult to recall characters, hold a guided reading session. Take time to talk, as a group, about what a character says and does at several points in the story. Ask the children to give an oral description of the character immediately after finishing the story to encourage their powers of recall.
Extension: Encourage the children to find key words in a text that describe a character and collect these for future writing.

Key aspects of learning
Evaluation: Children will discuss success criteria for their written work, give feedback to others and begin to judge the effectiveness of their own writing.
Communication: Children will develop their ability to discuss as they work collaboratively in paired, group and whole-class contexts. They will communicate outcomes orally, through writing and ICT if appropriate.

NARRATIVE

Phase ① Compare stories

Learning outcome
Children can compare stories and give preferences with reasons.

Success criteria
- I can remember a favourite story.
- I can compare stories.

Setting the context
This assessment should be undertaken after the children have listened to and read several stories with familiar settings in shared and guided reading sessions. The children should also have been introduced to the terms 'character', 'setting' and 'events'. Arrange the children into small groups and provide them with copies of three stories that have been read recently. Ask the children to tell you what they can recall about each of the stories. Encourage them to name the main characters, tell you where each story took place and what happens in each one. Afterwards, invite the children to say which of the three stories they enjoyed the most and give a reason.

Assessment opportunity
Provide the children with copies of the photocopiable page 'My favourite story' (version 1 or 2). Read the text on each page aloud to the children, before inviting them to write their own opinions. For children working at level 1, an adult can provide support by asking the children to describe what they want to say and scribing for them as appropriate. Children working at levels 2-3 can complete the photocopiable page independently. When they have completed the task, invite the children to read their pages aloud. Encourage them to expand on their responses by asking questions. For example, *Why do you like this story better than the other two? What did you like about the character? Is the setting like anywhere you know? What was your favourite part of the story? How did the story end?*

Assessment evidence
At level 1, the children will respond in writing with mostly single words but will be able to give fuller responses orally. At levels 2-3, the children's written responses should closely match their oral responses. Use the children's individual oral responses and completed photocopiable page to provide evidence against Reading AF6.

Next steps
Support: When reading stories with familiar settings, encourage the children to relate the setting and events to their own lives. This might include describing and comparing locations such as the school, home or playground.
Extension: Encourage the children to use the terms 'beginning', 'middle' and 'ending' when describing stories orally.

Key aspects of learning
Motivation: Children will have a clear goal for their independent writing – composing three complete sentences – and will be able to assess their own progress in achieving that goal as they read through what they have written.
Communication: Children will develop their ability to discuss as they work collaboratively in paired, group and whole-class contexts. They will communicate outcomes orally, in writing and through ICT if appropriate.

Phase ② Telling a story

Learning outcome
Children can sequence the main events of a story.

Success criteria
- I can retell a story.
- I can create a storyboard.

Setting the context
Prior to this assessment, the children should have had opportunities to discuss beginnings, middles and endings of stories that they have read. Display an enlarged copy of the photocopiable page 'Telling a story'. Ask the children to describe what they think is happening in each picture. Encourage them to contribute further detail to the pictures by suggesting who the characters are, what they are saying and how they might be feeling in each picture. Ask them to suggest what order the pictures should be in to show the beginning, middle and ending of a story.

Assessment opportunity
Provide the children with individual copies of the photocopiable page 'Telling a story'. Ask them to cut out the pictures and put them into the correct sequence. Then, invite them to glue the pictures onto a sheet of paper and write a sentence for each picture to tell the story. Children working at level 1 can sequence the pictures and give you a sentence for each one orally. A supporting adult can then help them to write the key words or sentences on their sheet. Alternatively, you can asses the children using the interactive activity 'Telling a story'. At levels 2-3, the children can complete the sentences independently. Afterwards, ask the children to read their stories aloud and encourage them to add further detail.

Assessment evidence
At level 1, the children should be able to sequence the story and provide key words for each picture. They may be able to attempt some sentences. At level 2, the children will be able to write sentences with basic time connectives. For example, 'then', 'next' and 'later'. At level 3, they will use more adventurous phrases to show the sequence. For example, 'one day', 'suddenly', 'they went home'. Use the children's oral responses, photocopiable pages and the completed interactive activity to provide evidence against Writing AF3.

Next steps
Support: For those children who struggled to put the pictures in order, use a writing frame in guided writing sessions which provides a clear beginning, middle and ending.
Extension: Encourage the children to add details to the sentences in guided writing sessions using adverbs and adjectives to describe the characters and events.

Key aspects of learning
Creative thinking: Children will apply imaginative ideas to create ideas for drama and story writing based on familiar incidents and settings.
Motivation: Children will have a clear goal for their independent writing - composing three complete sentences - and will be able to assess their own progress in achieving that goal as they read through what they have written.

NARRATIVE

Phase ② Performing a story

Learning outcome
Children can re-enact a story, sequencing the main events and using phrases from the text.

Success criteria
I can perform a story.

Setting the context
This assessment should be undertaken after the children have read and explored several stories with different, familiar settings. Remind the children of the stories they have listened to and read recently, and work together to draw up a list of these titles on the whiteboard. Choose three or four stories from the list and then talk together about the characters, settings and events that feature in each. Write the characters' names on the board. Arrange the children into groups of two or three and ask them to choose one of the stories from the board to act out. Provide time for the groups to plan their performance, discussing who will play which roles and how they will act out the story. Afterwards, ask each group to perform their story to the rest of the class.

Assessment opportunity
Observe the children as they plan their retelling of the story and make notes against the class list. Before the children perform their story, work together to draw up a short list of success criteria on the board. For example, *Does the story have a clear beginning, middle and ending? Can you tell who the characters are? Are the events in the right sequence?* Invite one group at a time to perform their retelling and then evaluate it against the success criteria. Ask the children to choose two things from the performance they think worked well and one thing that could be improved.

Assessment evidence
At level 1, the children should recall some of the events of their chosen story. At levels 2–3, the children will use more detail to retell the story and use some words and phrases remembered from the text. Use notes made against the class list and children's own assessments of the performances as evidence against Reading AF2.

Next steps
Support: Ask the children to draw a storyboard to help them retell the story in sequence.
Extension: Encourage the groups to write their own collaborative retelling of their chosen story.

Key aspects of learning
Creative thinking: Children will apply imaginative ideas to create ideas for drama and story writing based on familiar incidents and settings.
Evaluation: Children will discuss success criteria for their written work, give feedback to others and begin to judge the effectiveness of their own writing.
Communication: Children will develop their ability to discuss as they work collaboratively in paired, group and whole-class contexts. They will communicate outcomes orally, in writing and through ICT if appropriate.

Phase ③ Make up a story

Learning outcome
Children can write three simple sentences to tell a story.

Success criteria
I can write a story with three sentences.

Setting the context
Perform this assessment after the children have had the opportunity to contribute to a shared writing task. During a shared writing session, relate an event to the class about losing something. Describe what it was you lost, how you felt about losing it and how you found it again. Model how to use language that describes emotion. For example, 'worried', 'frightened', 'upset', 'unhappy', 'distraught', 'miserable'. Encourage the children to tell you about their own experiences of losing something. Draw up a list of words from the children's experiences to describe feelings. This activity can also be linked to *Developing Early Writing* (DfEE, 2001) Year 1 Unit 4.

Assessment opportunity
Provide the children with the photocopiable page 'Make up a story' (version 1 or 2). Ask them to illustrate and write three sentences about how they lost something, how they felt and how they found it again. At level 1, the children can use version 1 of the photocopiable page to sequence their feelings using the emotive faces, and then write a key word to describe each feeling. At levels 2–3, the children can use version 2 to draw their own pictures and write sentences to describe their feelings.

Assessment evidence
At level 1, the children will identify simple words to describe emotion such as 'sad', 'happy' and 'cross'. At levels 2–3, the children's vocabulary choices should to be more adventurous, with those at level 3 showing some use of adverbials to sequence their writing. For example, 'when I', 'after a while'. Use the children's independently written responses and the photocopiable pages to provide evidence against Writing AF1.

Next steps
Support: Help the children to write a list of synonyms for the words that they chose to describe their feelings. Invite them to add these new words to their personal word banks.
Extension: Encourage the children to write three short paragraphs instead of three single sentences for their story.

Key aspects of learning
Creative thinking: Children will apply imaginative ideas to create ideas for drama and story writing based on familiar incidents and settings.
Communication: Children will develop their ability to discuss as they work collaboratively in paired, group and whole-class contexts. They will communicate outcomes orally, in writing and through ICT if appropriate.

NARRATIVE

Periodic assessment

NARRATIVE

Reading

Learning outcome
Children can identify the main character and setting in a story using evidence from the illustrations and text.

Success criteria
I can listen to and talk about stories.

Setting the context
This assessment should be carried out once the children have completed the work from this unit. Explain to the children that you are going to read them a new story. (Suitable stories in big book format include, *Can't you Sleep Little Bear?* by Martin Waddell, *Asha in the Attic* by Chris Powling and *Not Now, Bernard* by David McKee). Share the story and, immediately on finishing it, read it through one more time. After the second reading, ask the following questions: *What is the setting of the story? Who is the main character? Which other characters are in the story? What is the first event? What happens in the middle? What happens at the end?* Make notes against the class list of the children's individual, oral responses.

Assessment opportunity
Write the three main events from the story on the board, using simple sentences, in a random order. Provide the children with copies of the photocopiable page 'Narrative 1 Reading assessment'. Invite them to complete it, reordering your sentences from the board.

Assessment evidence
At level 1, the children can write the title of the story and main character, and add key words to their drawings by making reference to your sentences on the board. At levels 2-3, the children will show more confidence in recalling the story and ordering the events. Use the children's written and oral responses to provide evidence against Reading AF2 and AF4.

MSCHOLASTIC

Periodic assessment

Writing

Learning outcome
Children can write three simple sentences to tell a story.

Success criteria
I can write a story with three simple sentences.

Setting the context
Collect the two pieces of written work completed during the course of this unit (see the Phase 2 activity 'Telling a story' and Phase 3 activity 'Make up a story') and discuss each child's achievements with them. Ask them what they found difficult and what they found easy when tackling the work in this unit. Make notes of their responses against the class list.

Assessment opportunity
Invite the children to choose the piece of writing that they think is the best, giving reasons for their choice. Invite them to re-read the story that they did not choose as their best and challenge them to add or re-write the sentences to improve it, and turn the piece into a finished story. When the children have completed their stories, ask them to say what they have done to improve the original piece of writing.

Assessment evidence
At level 1, the children will write simple sentences using key words and simple connectives such as 'and', 'but' and 'then'. At level 2, the children should make use of new vocabulary and vary the way they begin sentences. Children working at level 3 will use more complex sentences and vary their vocabulary choices for effect. Make comparisons between your own assessment of children's writing during this unit with their oral responses of their own achievements. This can be used to provide evidence against Writing AF5 and AF7.

NARRATIVE

Name	Date

My favourite character

Story: _____

Character name: _____

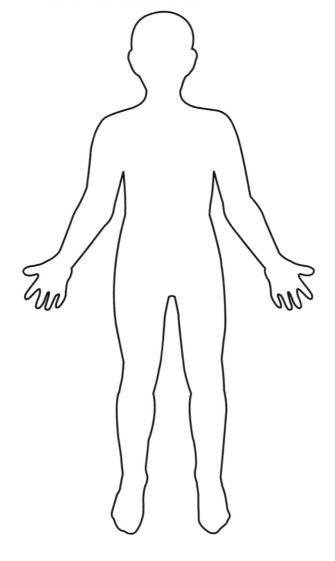

I like this character because _____

_____

_____

Red
Amber
Green

I can remember a character from a favourite story. ☐

Telling a story

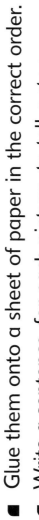

■ Cut out the pictures.

■ Glue them onto a sheet of paper in the correct order.

■ Write a sentence, for each picture, to tell a story.

Illustrations © 2010, Anna Godwin/The Illustrator Agency.

NARRATIVE

Name   Date

Make up a story (1)

- Choose a face for each sentence of the story.
- Draw the face in the box.
- Write a word that describes how you feel.

Last night I could not find my teddy.

I felt _____

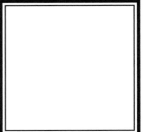

I looked everywhere for Teddy but I couldn't find him.

I felt _____

Suddenly I saw him in the dog basket, fast asleep with our dog!

I felt _____

Red
Amber
Green

I can write a story with three sentences. ☐

Name _____ Date _____

Narrative 1 Reading assessment

The story title is:

_____

The main character is:

_____

First event

_____

_____

_____

Second event

_____

_____

_____

Last event

_____

_____

_____

Red
Amber   I can listen to and talk about stories. ☐
Green

NARRATIVE
UNIT 2 Stories with predictable patterned language

Literacy objectives

Speak and listen for a wide range of purposes in different contexts
Strand 2 Listening and responding
● Listen with sustained concentration, building new stores of words in different contexts.

Read and write for a range of purposes on paper and on screen
Strand 5 Word recognition: decoding (reading) and encoding (spelling)
● Recognise and use alternative ways of pronouncing the graphemes already taught.
● Recognise and use alternative ways of spelling the phonemes already taught.
● Recognise automatically an increasing number of familiar high frequency words.
● Apply phonic knowledge and skills as the prime approach to reading and spelling unfamiliar words that are not completely decodable.
● Read more challenging texts which can be decoded using their acquired phonic knowledge and skills, along with automatic recognition of high frequency words.
Strand 7 Understanding and interpreting texts
● Identify the main events and characters in stories, and find specific information in simple texts.
● Use syntax and context when reading for meaning.
● Explore the effect of patterns of language and repeated words and phrases.
Strand 8 Engaging with and responding to texts
● Select books for personal reading and give reasons for choices.
Strand 9 Creating and shaping texts
● Independently choose what to write about, plan and follow it through.
● Use key features of narrative in their own writing.
● Find and use new and interesting words and phrases, including story language.
● Create short simple texts on paper and screen that combine words with images
Strand 10 Text structure and organisation
● Write chronological and non-chronological texts using simple structures.
Strand 11 Sentence structure and punctuation
● Compose and write simple sentences independently to communicate meaning.
● Use capital letters and full stops when punctuating simple sentences.

Key aspects of learning

Empathy
● Children will learn about other worlds and consider the thoughts, feelings and actions of characters.
Creative thinking
● Children will use their imaginations as they create new ways of using and extending familiar patterns in new stories.

Key aspects of learning (continued)

Communication
● Children will develop their ability to discuss as they work collaboratively in paired, group and whole-class contexts. They will communicate outcomes orally, in writing and through ICT if appropriate.

Assessment focuses

Reading
AF1 *(use a range of strategies, including accurate decoding of text, to read for meaning).*
AF2 *(understand, describe, select or retrieve information, events or ideas from texts and use quotation and reference to text).*
AF5 *(explain and comment on writers' use of language, including grammatical and literary features at word and sentence level).*

Writing
AF3 *(organise and present whole texts effectively, sequencing and structuring information, ideas and events).*
AF7 *(select appropriate and effective vocabulary).*

Speaking and listening
Listening and responding (listen with sustained concentration).

Resources

Sequence 1
Phase 1 and 2 activities
Photocopiable page, 'New sentences' (versions 1 and 2)
Phase 3 activities
Photocopiable page, 'Familiar and unfamiliar'
Phase 4 activities
Photocopiable page, 'Kitty Little and the Great Flood'
Interactive activity, 'Sequencing a story'
Photocopiable page, 'My storyboard' (versions 1 and 2)
Sequence 2
Phase 1 activities
Photocopiable page, 'The Gruffalo' (versions 1 and 2)
Interactive activity, 'The Gruffalo'
Phase 2 activities
Photocopiable page, 'Fantasy animals' (versions 1 and 2)
Phase 3 activities
Photocopiable page, 'Book review'
Recommended texts
'The Gingerbread Man'; 'The Enormous Turnip'; *Mrs Wishy-Washy* by Joy Cowley (ISBN 978-0868-67044-7); *A Drop of Rain* by Wong Herbert Yee (ISBN 978-0395-71549-9); *Catch That Goat* by Polly Alakija (ISBN 978-1846-86056-0); *We're Riding on a Caravan* by Laurie Krebs (ISBN 978-1846-86107-9); T*he Gruffalo* by Julia Donaldson (ISBN 978-0333-71093-7); *The Other Ark* by Lynley Dodd (ISBN 978-0141-50018-8)

Unit 2 ▢ Stories with predictable patterned language

Learning outcomes	Assessment opportunity and evidence	Assessment focuses (AFs)	Success criteria
		Level 1	

Sequence 1

**Phase ① and ② ** activity page 31

| **Patterned language** • Children can recognise language patterns and repeated words and phrases in a text and discuss their effect on a reader. • Children can write their own sentences based on patterned language from a familiar text. | • Independent and paired activity where children recite the repeated and patterned language in a story and use it to complete a series of sentences. • Children's completed photocopiable page, paired feedback and oral responses. | **Reading AF5** Comments on obvious features of language.

Writing AF7 • Mostly simple vocabulary. • Communicates meaning through repetition of key words. | • I can explore stories with patterned language. • I can write sentences that follow a pattern. |

**Phase ③ ** activity page 32

| **Familiar and unfamiliar** Children can work as part of a group, taking turns sharing ideas, listening to others and reporting their findings. | • Group activity where children explore the familiar and unfamiliar aspects of a story from another culture. • Children's completed photocopiable page and oral responses. | **Reading AF2** • Some simple points from familiar texts recalled. • Some pages/sections of interest located. | I can talk about familiar and unfamiliar features of a book. |

**Phase ④ ** activity page 33

| **Planning a story** Children can write simple sentences using patterned language, words and phrases taken from familiar stories. | • Independent activity where children sequence a story and create their own storyboard plan. • Children's completed interactive activity and storyboard notes on the photocopiable page. | **Writing AF3** • Some formulaic phrases indicate start/end of text. • Events/ideas sometimes in appropriate order. | • I can use written notes to plan a story. • I can write a story using patterned language. |

Sequence 2

**Phase ① ** activity page 34

| **Rhymes** Children can recognise language patterns and repeated words and phrases in a text and discuss their effect on a reader. | • Independent activity where children identify rhyming words in an extract from *The Gruffalo*. • Children's oral responses, completed photocopiable page and/ or interactive activity. | **Reading AF1** • Some high frequency and familiar words read fluently and automatically. • Decode familiar and some unfamiliar words using blending as the prime approach. • Some awareness of punctuation marks. | • I can find rhymes in a story. • I can find repeated words and sentences in a story. |

**Phase ② ** activity page 35

| **Fantasy creatures** Children can write their own sentences based on patterned language from a familiar text. | • Paired and independent activity where children invent the name of a fantasy animal and write five lines about it. • Children's completed photocopiable pages and peer assessment. | **Writing AF7** • Mostly simple vocabulary. • Communicates meaning through repetition of key words. | • I can make up a name for a character. • I can write a story using patterned language. |

Unit 2 📖 Stories with predictable patterned language

Learning outcomes	Assessment opportunity and evidence	Assessment focuses (AFs)	Success criteria
		Level 1	

Phase ③ activity page 36

Learning outcomes	Assessment opportunity and evidence	Assessment focuses (AFs) Level 1	Success criteria
Comparing stories from another culture Children can work as part of a group, taking turns sharing ideas, listening to others and reporting their findings.	• Group activity where children find familiar and unfamiliar aspects of a story from another culture and report their findings to the class. • Group discussion and oral presentations. • Children's oral contributions to the discussion and peer feedback.	**Reading AF2** • Some simple points from familiar texts recalled. • Some pages/sections of interest located.	I can talk about familiar and unfamiliar features of a book.

Phase ④ activity page 37

Learning outcomes	Assessment opportunity and evidence	Assessment focuses (AFs) Level 1	Success criteria
Writing the middle of a story Children can write simple sentences using patterned language, words and phrases taken from familiar stories.	• Independent activity where children write the middle section of a story. • Children's completed story sections and oral responses.	**Writing AF7** • Mostly simple vocabulary. • Communicates meaning through repetition of key words.	• I can use a familiar story as a model for planning a new story. • I can write a story using patterned language. • I can write the middle of a story.

Learning outcomes	Assessment opportunity and evidence	Assessment focuses (AFs)		Success criteria
		Level 2	Level 3	

Sequence 1

Phase ① and ② activity page 31

Learning outcomes	Assessment opportunity and evidence	Level 2	Level 3	Success criteria
Patterned language • Children can recognise language patterns and repeated words and phrases in a text and discuss their effect on a reader. • Children can write their own sentences based on patterned language from a familiar text.	• Independent and paired activity where children recite the repeated and patterned language in a story and use it to complete a series of sentences. • Children's completed photocopiable page, paired feedback and oral responses.	**Reading AF5** • Some effective language choices noted. • Some familiar patterns of language identified. **Writing AF7** • Simple, often speech-like vocabulary conveys relevant meanings. • Some adventurous word choices.	**Reading AF5** A few basic features of writer's use of language identified, but with little or no comment. **Writing AF7** • Simple, generally appropriate vocabulary used, limited in range. • Some words selected for effect or occasion.	• I can explore stories with patterned language. • I can write sentences that follow a pattern.

Phase ③ activity page 32

Learning outcomes	Assessment opportunity and evidence	Level 2	Level 3	Success criteria
Familiar and unfamiliar Children can work as part of a group, taking turns sharing ideas, listening to others and reporting their findings.	• Group activity where children explore the familiar and unfamiliar aspects of a story from another culture. • Children's completed photocopiable page and oral responses.	**Reading AF2** • Some specific, straightforward information recalled. • Generally clear idea of where to look for information.	**Reading AF2** • Simple, most obvious points identified though there may also be some misunderstanding. • Some comments include quotations from or references to text, but not always relevant.	I can talk about familiar and unfamiliar features of a book.

Unit 2 ▢ Stories with predictable patterned language

Learning outcomes	Assessment opportunity and evidence	Assessment focuses (AFs)		Success criteria
		Level 2	Level 3	
Phase ④ activity page 33				
Planning a story Children can write simple sentences using patterned language, words and phrases taken from familiar stories.	● Independent activity where children sequence sections of a story and create their own storyboard plan. ● Children's completed interactive activity and storyboard notes.	**Writing AF3** ● Some basic sequencing of ideas or material. ● Openings and/or closings sometimes signalled.	**Writing AF3** ● Some attempt to organise ideas with related points placed next to each other. ● Openings and closings usually signalled. ● Some attempt to sequence ideas or material logically.	● I can use written notes to plan a story. ● I can write a story using patterned language.
Sequence 2				
Phase ① activity page 34				
Rhymes Children can recognise language patterns and repeated words and phrases in a text and discuss their effect on a reader.	● Independent activity where children identify rhyming words in an extract from *The Gruffalo*. ● Children's oral responses, completed photocopiable page and/ or interactive activity.	**Reading AF1** ● Range of key words read on sight. ● Unfamiliar words decoded using appropriate strategies. ● Some fluency and expression.	**Reading AF1** Range of strategies used mostly effectively to read with fluency, understanding and expression.	● I can find rhymes in a story. ● I can find repeated words and sentences in a story.
Phase ② activity page 35				
Fantasy creatures Children can write their own sentences based on patterned language from a familiar text.	● Paired and independent activity where children invent the name of a fantasy animal and write five lines about it. ● Children's completed photocopiable pages and peer assessment.w	**Writing AF7** ● Simple, often speech-like vocabulary conveys relevant meanings. ● Some adventurous word choices.	**Writing AF7** ● Simple, generally appropriate vocabulary used, limited in range. ● Some words selected for effect or occasion.	● I can make up a name for a character. ● I can write a story using patterned language.
Phase ③ activity page 36				
Comparing stories from another culture Children can work as part of a group, taking turns sharing ideas, listening to others and reporting their findings.	● Group activity where children find familiar and unfamiliar aspects of a story from another culture and report their findings to the class. ● Group discussion and oral presentation of the group's findings. ● Children's oral contributions to the discussion and peer feedback.	**Reading AF2** ● Some specific, straightforward information recalled. ● Generally clear idea of where to look for information.	**Reading AF2** ● Simple, most obvious points identified though there may also be some misunderstanding. ● Some comments include quotations from or references to text, but not always relevant.	I can talk about familiar and unfamiliar features of a book.
Phase ④ activity page 37				
Writing the middle of a story Children can write simple sentences using patterned language, words and phrases taken from familiar stories.	● Independent activity where children write the middle section of a story. ● Children's completed story sections and oral responses.	**Writing AF7** ● Simple, often speech-like vocabulary conveys relevant meanings. ● Some adventurous word choices.	**Writing AF7** ● Simple, generally appropriate vocabulary used, limited in range. ● Some words selected for effect or occasion.	● I can use a familiar story as a model for planning a new story. ● I can write a story using patterned language. ● I can write the middle of a story

Phase ① and ② Patterned language

Learning outcomes
● Children can recognise language patterns and repeated words and phrases in a text and discuss their effect on a reader.
● Children can write their own sentences based on patterned language from a familiar text.

Success criteria
● I can explore stories with patterned language.
● I can write sentences that follow a pattern.

Setting the context
This assessment should be carried out once the children have read and explored several stories with predictable, patterned and repetitive language. They should also have explored writing sentences based on the characters, events and the patterned language from the stories. Read a story that is familiar to the children. For example, 'The Gingerbread Man', 'The Enormous Turnip' or *Mrs Wishy-Washy*. Ask the children to identify any repeated words, phrases or sentences, and discuss how some repeated sentences vary. Re-read the story and encourage the children to join in with the repetitions.

Assessment opportunity
Provide the children with the photocopiable page 'New sentences' (version 1 or 2). Ask the children to complete the three sentences and add a new one of their own. At level 1, the children should work on version 1 of the photocopiable page. At levels 2–3, the children should work on version 2. Afterwards, invite the children to swap their pages with a partner and then read their page aloud. Ask them to say which words their partner used that are repeated.

Assessment evidence
At level 1, the children will add some of the repeated words to the photocopiable page. At levels 2–3, the children will add the missing words to the sentences and create a complete, new sentence using the patterned language. The completed photocopiable pages and children's oral responses will provide evidence towards Reading AF5 and Writing AF7.

Next steps
Support: Provide the children with further stories that have repeated and patterned language, and work together to identify the refrains and repetitions.
Extension: Encourage the children to choose a favourite story that uses patterned language and invent a new line or lines that follow the same pattern.

Key aspects of learning
Creative thinking: Children will use their imaginations as they create new ways of using and extending familiar patterns in new stories.
Communication: Children will develop their ability to discuss as they work collaboratively in paired, group and whole-class contexts. They will communicate outcomes orally, in writing and through ICT if appropriate.

NARRATIVE

Phase ③ Familiar and unfamiliar

Learning outcome
Children can work as part of a group, taking turns sharing ideas, listening to others and reporting their findings.

Success criteria
I can talk about familiar and unfamiliar features of a book.

Setting the context
Perform this assessment once the children have studied a series of patterned stories from or about another culture, and have had the opportunity to explore what is familiar and what is unfamiliar about stories from other cultures. In groups, provide the children with copies of a new story from another culture. Suitable examples include: *A Drop of Rain* by Wong Herbert Yee, *Catch That Goat* by Polly Alakija and *We're Riding on a Caravan* by Laurie Krebs. Ask them to read the story and study the illustrations to find out what is familiar and different about the story compared with their own lives. Explain that they should talk to each other and compare their ideas before noting them down on their own copy of the photocopiable page 'Familiar and unfamiliar'. Ask them to also write down any language patterns they notice or words and phrases that they find interesting.

Assessment opportunity
Ask the groups to use their page of notes to give feedback about their findings. Draw out their responses with questioning. For example, *What else about the setting is the same as or different from your home/town?* Make notes of their oral responses. Invite each member of the group to assess their own and others' contributions to the discussion. What points did they make? Which words or phrases did they find?

Assessment evidence
At level 1, the children should be able to identify and write down key words and phrases from the text. At levels 2–3, the children will identify familiarities and differences, and note these in their own words and/or using phrases from the text. The children's completed photocopiable pages and oral responses will provide evidence against Reading AF2.

Next steps
Support: For groups that experienced difficulty in discussing the text, arrange them into mixed-ability groups and discuss a different text. Ensure that they each take a turn to contribute to the discussion.
Extension: In guided reading sessions, invite the children to describe in more depth how settings, characters and events are similar or different to their own lives, giving reasons and examples to support their ideas.

Key aspects of learning
Empathy: Children will learn about other worlds and consider the thoughts, feelings and actions of characters.
Communication: Children will develop their ability to discuss as they work collaboratively in paired, group and whole-class contexts. They will communicate outcomes orally, in writing and through ICT if appropriate.

Phase ④ Planning a story

Learning outcome
Children can write simple sentences using patterned language, words and phrases taken from familiar stories.

Success criteria
- I can use written notes to plan a story.
- I can write a story using patterned language.

Setting the context
This assessment should be carried out after the children have explored stories that use repeated and patterned language. They should also have had experience of planning a story with repeated language using a storyboard. Display a selection of the stories the children have been reading during the course of this unit. Invite the children to choose one to form the basis of a new story. Remind them how to make notes on a storyboard using a re-worked version of *Chicken Licken* ('Kitty Little and the Great Flood'), on the photocopiable page. Ask the children to point out any similarities and differences.

Assessment opportunity
Invite the children to sequence a storyboard using the interactive activity 'Sequencing a story'. When the children have completed the activity, ask them to describe how they went about choosing sections and ordering their story. They should make reference to the build up of characters, the use of repeated words and phrases like *one day* and *the farmer never knew* to denote the start and end of the story. Afterwards, provide the children with copies of the photocopiable page 'My storyboard' (version 1 or 2) and invite them to make notes for their new story based on their chosen text.

Assessment evidence
At level 1, the children will draw and write key words on version 1 of the photocopiable page. At levels 2–3, the children will use version 2 of the photocopiable page and make notes using key words, phrases and sentences. Use the completed interactive activity, photocopiable pages and children's oral responses to provide evidence against Writing AF3.

Next steps
Support: Use a guided writing session and the children's storyboards to help them expand their notes to include sentences for the story.
Extension: Encourage the children to use their storyboards to write a complete version of their story.

Key aspects of learning
Creative thinking: Children will use their imaginations as they create new ways of using and extending familiar patterns in new stories.
Communication: Children will develop their ability to discuss as they work collaboratively in paired, group and whole-class contexts. They will communicate outcomes orally, in writing and through ICT if appropriate.

Phase ① Rhymes

Learning outcome
Children can recognise language patterns and repeated words and phrases in a text and discuss their effect on a reader.

Success criteria
- I can find rhymes in a story.
- I can find repeated words and sentences in a story.

Setting the context
This assessment should be undertaken once the children have explored stories with patterned language and rhyming words. Read a rhyming story with the children such as *The Gruffalo* by Julia Donaldson. Look back at one or two of the pages and ask the children to identify the words on the pages that rhyme and any examples of repetition.

Assessment opportunity
Provide the children with the photocopiable page 'The Gruffalo' (version 1 for those at level 1; version 2 for those at levels 2-3). Ask them to use different coloured pencils to circle the rhyming words in the text. Then, invite them to identify other rhyming words from either the list at the side (version 1) or the word box at the foot of the page (version 2). Alternatively, the children can complete the interactive activity 'The Gruffalo' by highlighting the rhyming words. Afterwards, ask the children to tell you how they recognised the words that rhymed. Did they find any words that rhyme but have different spelling patterns? (For example: *no/gruffalo/ know; rocks/fox; jaws/roars/doors.*) Ask the children to identify any words that are repeated in this extract from the story (*mouse, fox, gruffalo, terrible*). How does word repetition add to the humorous effect of the story? Make notes of the children's oral responses against the class list.

Assessment evidence
At level 1, the children will recognise some key words from sight and attempt to blend unfamiliar words to hear what they sound like. At levels 2-3, the children will use a range of strategies, including knowledge of sight vocabulary, segmenting and blending the sounds and predicting words that make sense. The children's oral responses, completed photocopiable pages and/or interactive activity will provide evidence against Reading AF1.

Next steps
Support: For the children who have difficulty in hearing the rhymes in words, provide them with rhyming CVC and CVCC word cards in guided reading sessions and ask them to read and match the cards that rhyme.
Extension: Invite the children to make a list of words that rhyme with those in the text.

Key aspects of learning
Creative thinking: Children will use their imaginations as they create new ways of using and extending familiar patterns in new stories.
Communication: Children will develop their ability to discuss as they work collaboratively in paired, group and whole-class contexts. They will communicate outcomes orally, in writing and through ICT if appropriate.

Phase ② Fantasy creatures

Learning outcome
Children can write their own sentences based on patterned language from a familiar text.

Success criteria
- I can make up a name for a character.
- I can write a story using patterned language.

Setting the context
Perform this assessment once the children have explored a variety of texts that use rhyme, repetition and invented names for characters. Examples include *The Gruffalo* by Julia Donaldson and *The Other Ark* by Lynley Dodd. They should also have explored how authors have created creatures by mixing up the names of animals. For example, the name 'alligatiger' from *The Other Ark* is made by joining 'alligator' with 'tiger'. Explain to the children that they are going to invent an animal for a story and write sentences for their new story.

Assessment opportunity
Together, create a list of known animals on the board. In pairs, provide the children with a blank sheet of paper and ask them to work together to create a fantasy animal by combining two names from the list. Encourage them to experiment until they have created a name that they both agree on. Ask them to add labels to describe the features of their new animal and any imaginative adjectives they associate with it. Afterwards, hand out the photocopiable page 'Fantasy animals' (version 1 for those at level 1; version 2 for those at levels 2–3). Ask the children, individually, to fill in the spaces on the page to write a story about their imaginary animal. When the children have completed the lines for their story, ask them to read them aloud for the other children. Invite them to say which invented names were the most effective and choose the lines they think worked well, giving reasons for their choices.

Assessment evidence
Use the children's oral responses and completed photocopiable pages as evidence against Writing AF7.

Next steps
Support: Discuss the children's descriptions and work together to improve them by exploring more effective adjectives.
Extension: Invite the children to write further lines for their story without sentence prompts.

Key aspects of learning
Creative thinking: Children will use their imaginations as they create new ways of using and extending familiar patterns in new stories.
Communication: Children will develop their ability to discuss as they work collaboratively in paired, group and whole-class contexts. They will communicate outcomes orally, in writing and through ICT if appropriate.

Phase ③ Comparing stories from another culture

Learning outcome
Children can work as part of a group, taking turns sharing ideas, listening to others and reporting their findings.

Success criteria
I can talk about familiar and unfamiliar features of a book.

Setting the context
This assessment should be performed once the children have studied a selection of stories from another culture. They should have discussed what is familiar and unfamiliar about the settings, characters, events and language in the stories. Arrange the children into small ability groups. Provide each group with a copy of a new story from another culture at an appropriate level for the group. If possible, give different titles to each of the groups. Ask them to read the text and study the illustrations to find out what is familiar and unfamiliar about the story compared with their own lives. Explain that they should talk to each other and compare their ideas before noting them down on a sheet of paper. Ask them to also write down any language patterns they notice or words and phrases that they find interesting.

Assessment opportunity
Ask one member from each of the groups to use their page of notes to give feedback about their findings. Encourage them to say what or how the other members of the group contributed to the discussion. Encourage them to compare what was similar and different about the stories read by other groups. Ask them to say if there are any aspects of these stories that are consistent.

Assessment evidence
At level 1, the children will contribute orally to the discussion. They will write key words about the familiar and unfamiliar aspects and phrases from the text. At levels 2-3, the children will describe their findings and ideas using their own words, as well as phrases from the text. Use the children's oral responses and written notes to provide evidence against Reading AF2.

Next steps
Support: For groups that experienced difficulty in discussing the text, give them headings to look out for when reading a similar text in guided reading. The photocopiable page 'Book review' can be used as a prompt.
Extension: Invite the children to use their group notes to write a book review about the title they discussed, using the photocopiable page 'Book review'.

Key aspects of learning
Empathy: Children will learn about other worlds and consider the thoughts, feelings and actions of characters.

Phase ④ Writing the middle of a story

Learning outcome
Children can write simple sentences using patterned language, words and phrases taken from familiar stories.

Success criteria
● I can use a familiar story as a model for planning a new story.
● I can write a story using patterned language.
● I can write the middle of a story.

Setting the context
This assessment should be carried out once the children have planned stories with a beginning, middle and ending in shared and guided writing sessions. Choose a story with patterned words and phrases that the children are already familiar with. Prepare a story outline with a beginning and ending based on the chosen story but with characters and events slightly altered. Discuss the similarities and differences between your new version and the original story and invite the children to write a middle section for the story.

Assessment opportunity
Allow time for the children to refer back to the original story for ideas and to make notes before writing their middle section. When the children have finished their middle sections, read together the beginning of your prepared outline and then invite the children to read their middle part before you read the ending. Discuss the children's individual contributions and ask them to evaluate which middle sections worked well with the story outline and how others could be improved. Make notes of their feedback against the class list.

Assessment evidence
At level 1, the children will use simple vocabulary with repetition and minimal reference to the stories they have been reading. At levels 2–3, the children should have used complete sentences, and used words and phrases from the stories they have been reading. Use the children's evaluations and their story sections to provide evidence against Writing AF7.

Next steps
Support: Read the story again and revisit the story outline. Ask the children to tell the middle part of the story orally, making more use of the original story's language patterns.
Extension: Invite the children to write a beginning and an ending for their middle section.

Key aspects of learning
Creative thinking: Children will use their imaginations as they create new ways of using and extending familiar patterns in new stories.
Communication: Children will develop their ability to discuss as they work collaboratively in paired, group and whole-class contexts. They will communicate outcomes orally, in writing and through ICT if appropriate.

Unit 2 ◻ **Stories with predictable patterned language**

Periodic assessment

Reading

Learning outcome
Children can recognise language patterns and repeated words and phrases in a text and discuss their effect on a reader.

Success criteria
● I can explore stories with patterned language.
● I can recognise rhymes and repetition in a story.

Setting the context
Work with the children in small groups to discuss the stories that have been read during the course of this unit. Ask the group to say what aspects of the stories they enjoyed most and to describe the features of the stories that make them different from other stories they have read before. Encourage them to say what they liked about the stories and what they disliked, as well as what they found hard about the work and what they found easy. Make notes of their responses against the class list.

Assessment opportunity
This assessment provides the opportunity for the children to evaluate their own understanding of the features of stories with predictable and patterned language and stories from other cultures.

Assessment evidence
At level 1, the children should recognise repeated phrases and rhyme and draw simple comparisons about how their lives differ from those depicted in the stories from other cultures. At levels 2–3, the children will recognise rhyme and repetition and identify familiar and unfamiliar characters, settings and events. Use the children's oral responses and notes completed during the course of the unit to provide evidence against Reading AF5.

Writing

Learning outcome
Children can write simple sentences using patterned language, words and phrases taken from familiar stories.

Success criteria
● I can use a familiar story as a model for planning a new story.
● I can write a story using patterned and repeated language.
● I can write the middle of a story.

Setting the context
Collect the work that has been completed during the course of this unit and discuss children's achievements with them. Ask them to suggest what they found difficult about the writing in the unit and what they found easy to accomplish. Make notes of their responses against the class list.

Assessment opportunity
Ask the children to choose a piece of writing that they feel represents their best work. Ask them to swap with a partner. Tell them to read their partner's work and describe two things they have done well and one thing that might improve it. Invite them to revise their own writing, taking into account what they have learned during the whole unit and their partner's comments.

Assessment evidence
The children's oral responses and peer evaluations can be used to provide evidence against Writing AF1. Make notes of how children's self- and partner evaluations differ from your own evaluations and plan appropriate action for the next unit.

Name	Date

New sentences (1)

Fill in the words to complete the sentences.

In went _____

_____

wishy washy, wishy washy.

In went _____

_____

wishy washy, wishy washy.

In _____

_____

wishy washy, wishy washy.

In _____

_____

wishy washy, _____.

Red
Amber
Green

I can explore stories with patterned language. ☐
I can write sentences that follow a pattern. ☐

NARRATIVE

NARRATIVE

Kitty Little and the Great Flood

One day Kitty Little was walking through the farm when suddenly she fell into a puddle. It went right up to her middle!

"Oh no!" cried Kitty Little. "The farm is flooding. I must run and tell the farmer."

So off she ran as fast as she could go. On the way she met her friend Dilly Duckling.

"Oh Dilly Duckling," cried Kitty Little. "I fell into a puddle right up to my middle. The farm is flooding. We must run and tell the farmer."

So Kitty Little and Dilly Duckling ran off as fast as they could go. On the way Kitty Little and Dilly Duckling met Butch, the sheepdog.

"Now where are you off to in such a hurry?" he asked.

"Oh sir!" cried Kitty Little and Dilly Duckling at once. "The farm is flooding. We must run and tell the farmer."

"I fell into a puddle right up to my middle!" added Kitty Little in case Butch did not understand.

Butch looked around and then shook his head.

"What rubbish!" he said.

So Butch barked such a loud bark that Kitty Little and Dilly Duckling ran all the way back home and the farmer never knew the farm was flooding.

Text © 2010, Gillian Howell. Illustration © 2010, Anna Godwin/The Illustrator Agency.

Name	Date

The Gruffalo (1)

◾ Draw a circle round the words that rhyme. Use different colours for each different rhyme.

◾ Then, draw a line to the word that rhymes on the side of the page.

A mouse took a stroll through the deep dark wood.

A fox saw the mouse and the mouse looked good.

"Where are you going to, little brown mouse?

Come and have lunch in my underground house."

"It's terribly kind of you, Fox, but no —

I'm going to have lunch with a gruffalo."

blow

paws

"A gruffalo? What's a gruffalo?"

"A gruffalo! Why, didn't you know?

box

"He has terrible tusks, and terrible claws,

And terrible teeth in his terrible jaws."

hood

"Where are you meeting him?"

"Here, by these rocks,

And his favourite food is roasted fox."

slow

Red
Amber
Green

I can find rhymes in a story. ▢

I can find repeated words and sentences in a story. ▢

NARRATIVE
UNIT 3 Traditional and fairy tales

Literacy objectives

Speak and listen for a wide range of purposes in different contexts
Strand 1 Speaking
- Retell stories, ordering events using story language.

Strand 2 Listening and responding
- Listen to tapes or video and express views about how a story has been presented.

Strand 4 Drama
- Explore familiar themes and characters through improvisation and role play.
- Act out their own and well-known stories, using voices for characters.

Read and write for a range of purposes on paper and on screen
Strand 5 Word recognition: decoding (reading) and encoding (spelling)
- Identify the constituent parts of two-syllable and three-syllable words to support the application of phonic knowledge and skills.
- Recognise automatically an increasing number of familiar high frequency words.
- Apply phonic knowledge and skills as the prime approach to reading and spelling unfamiliar words that are not completely decodable.
- Read and spell phonically decodable two-syllable and three-syllable words.

Strand 7 Understanding and interpreting texts
- Identify the main events and characters in stories, and find specific information in simple texts.
- Use syntax and context when reading for meaning.
- Recognise the main elements that shape different texts.

Strand 8 Engaging with and responding to texts
- Select books for personal reading and give reasons for choices.
- Visualise and comment on events, characters and ideas, making imaginative links to their own experiences.

Strand 9 Creating and shaping texts
- Use key features of narrative in their own writing.
- Find and use new and interesting words and phrases, including story language.
- Create short simple texts on paper and screen that combine words with images.

Strand 10 Text structure and organisation
- Write chronological and non-chronological texts using simple structures.
- Group written sentences together in chunks of meaning or subject.

Strand 11 Sentence structure and punctuation
- Compose and write simple sentences independently to communicate meaning.

Key aspects of learning

Reasoning
- Children will have opportunities to compare different versions of stories, to express their opinions and make judgements about which they prefer.

Creative thinking
- Children will respond imaginatively to character descriptions, exploring motives and behaviour through role play.

Key aspects of learning (continued)

Empathy
- Children will consider the thoughts, feelings and actions of characters in stories.

Social skills
- Children will learn about taking turns, listening to others and trying to reach agreement as they work together in a group.

Communication
- Children will develop their ability to speak before an audience as they tell stories for a group.

Evaluation
- Children will listen to one another's oral and written stories and give feedback about specific aspects.

Assessment focuses

Reading

AF1 *(use a range of strategies, including accurate decoding of text, to read for meaning).*
AF2 *(understand, describe, select or retrieve information, events or ideas from texts and use quotation and reference to text).*
AF6 *(identify and comment on writers' purposes and viewpoints).*

Writing

AF1 *(write imaginative, interesting and thoughtful texts).*
AF7 *(select appropriate and effective vocabulary).*

Speaking and listening

Speaking (speak with clarity, intonation and pace).
Listening and responding (respond appropriately).
Drama (improvise and sustain role).

Resources

Phase 1 activities
Photocopiable page, 'Jumbled sentences' (versions 1 and 2)
Interactive activity, 'Goldilocks and the Three Bears'
Phase 2 activities
Photocopiable page, 'Story props'
Phase 3 activities
Photocopiable page, 'Character profile' (versions 1 and 2)
Phase 4 activities
Photocopiable page, 'The Three Billy Goats Gruff' (versions 1 and 2)
Phase 5 activities
Photocopiable page, 'Stick puppets'
Phase 6 activities
Photocopiable page, 'The Princess and the Pea'
Interactive activity, 'The Princess and the Pea'
Photocopiable page, 'Story plan' (versions 1 and 2)
Recommended texts *Goldilocks and the Three Bears* by Lauren Child (ISBN 978-0141383309); *The Three Billy Goats Gruff* by Mary Finch (978-1841483511); *The Three Billy Goats Gruff – a play* from *Play Time!* by Julia Donaldson (ISBN 978-0330445955).

Unit 3 ▢ Traditional and fairy tales

Learning outcomes	Assessment opportunity and evidence	Assessment focuses (AFs)	Success criteria
		Level 1	
Phase ① activity page 47			
Goldilocks and the Three Bears Children can identify the main events in traditional tales, sequencing them in chronological order.	• Paired activity where children cut out and sequence sentences to retell the story of 'Goldilocks and the Three Bears'. • Partner discussion and retelling of the sequenced story. • Children's sequenced stories and completed interactive activity.	**Reading AF2** • Some simple points from familiar texts recalled. • Some pages/sections of interest located.	• I can retell a traditional tale. • I can retell a traditional tale by sorting jumbled sentences.
Phase ② activity page 48			
Story props Children can retell a traditional familiar story in chronological order using story language.	• Independent and group activity where children use images and props to retell a story using traditional story language. • Group discussion and feedback on each retelling. • Children's performances and oral responses.	**Writing AF7** • Mostly simple vocabulary. • Communicates meaning through repetition of key words.	• I can compare traditional tales. • I can use puppets and props to retell a story.
Phase ③ activity page 49			
Characters • Children can discuss the appearance, behaviour, characteristics and goals of characters. • Children can write a profile of a character using visual and written text.	• Independent and paired activity where children create a character profile and then swap it with a partner to guess who the character is and which story they come from. • Partner discussion and feedback on the effectiveness of the profiles. • Children's completed photocopiable page and oral responses.	**Reading AF2** • Some simple points from familiar texts recalled. • Some pages/sections of interest located.	• I can describe the characters in a traditional story. • I can write a character profile.
Phase ④ activity page 50			
The Three Billy Goats Gruff Children can discuss how narratives on audio tape or video are presented and express an opinion about the different versions.	• Supported group activity where children read, listen to and/or watch two versions of 'The Three Billy Goats Gruff', compare them and express their preferences. • Supported group discussion. • Children's completed photocopiable pages and oral responses.	**Reading AF6** Some simple comments about preferences, mostly linked to own experience.	• I can explore a different version of a story. • I can say which version of a story I like best.

Unit 3 ☐ Traditional and fairy tales

Learning outcomes	Assessment opportunity and evidence	Assessment focuses (AFs) Level 1	Success criteria
Phase ⑤ activity page 51			
Three Billy Goats Gruff – a play Children can say what a playscript is for and can identify some ways in which it differs from a story text.	• Group activity where children read a playscript and work out their own role play performance using stick puppets. • Group discussion and planning of the performance. • Children's oral feedback and self/peer evaluations.	**Reading AF6** Some simple comments about preferences, mostly linked to own experience.	• I can compare a book and a play version of a story. • I can explore a play version of a story. • I can retell a story using puppets.
Phase ⑥ activity page 52			
Writing the story Children can write their own version of a traditional story, using a series of complete sentences organised into chronological order.	• Paired activity where children sequence a story, matching images to text, and then plan and write their own version of the story. • Paired discussion while completing the interactive activity and planning the story. • Children's completed story plans, written stories and peer evaluations.	**Reading AF1** • Some high frequency and familiar words read fluently and automatically. • Decode familiar and some unfamiliar words using blending as the prime approach. • Some awareness of punctuation marks. **Writing AF1** • Basic information and ideas conveyed through appropriate word choice. • Some descriptive language.	• I can retell a traditional story in my own words. • I can write a story plan. • I can write my own version of a traditional story.

Learning outcomes	Assessment opportunity and evidence	Assessment focuses (AFs)		Success criteria
		Level 2	Level 3	
Phase ① activity page 47				
Goldilocks and the Three Bears Children can identify the main events in traditional tales, sequencing them in chronological order.	• Paired activity where children cut out and sequence sentences to retell the story of 'Goldilocks and the Three Bears'. • Partner discussion and retelling of the sequenced story. • Children's sequenced stories and completed interactive activity.	**Reading AF2** • Some specific, straightforward information recalled. • Generally clear idea of where to look for information.	**Reading AF2** • Simple, most obvious points identified though there may also be some misunderstanding. • Some comments include quotations from or references to text, but not always relevant.	• I can retell a traditional tale. • I can retell a traditional tale by sorting jumbled sentences.
Phase ② activity page 48				
Story props Children can retell a traditional familiar story in chronological order using story language.	• Independent and group activity where children use images and props to retell a story using traditional story language. • Group discussion and feedback on each retelling. • Children's performances and oral responses.	**Writing AF7** • Simple, often speech-like vocabulary conveys relevant meanings. • Some adventurous word choices.	**Writing AF7** • Simple, generally appropriate vocabulary used, limited in range. • Some words selected for effect or occasion.	• I can compare traditional tales. • I can use puppets and props to retell a story.

Unit 3 ▭ Traditional and fairy tales

Learning outcomes	Assessment opportunity and evidence	Assessment focuses (AFs)		Success criteria
		Level 2	Level 3	
Phase ③ activity page 49				
Characters • Children can discuss the appearance, behaviour, characteristics and goals of characters. • Children can write a profile of a character using visual and written text.	• Independent and paired activity where children create a character profile for two storybook characters and then swap it with a partner to guess who the characters are and which stories they come from. • Partner discussion and feedback on the effectiveness of the profiles. • Children's completed photocopiable page and oral responses.	**Reading AF2** • Some specific, straightforward information recalled. • Generally clear idea of where to look for information.	**Reading AF2** • Simple, most obvious points identified though there may also be some misunderstanding. • Some comments include quotations from or references to text, but not always relevant.	• I can describe the characters in a traditional story. • I can write a character profile.
Phase ④ activity page 50				
The Three Billy Goats Gruff Children can discuss how narratives on audio tape or video are presented and express an opinion about the different versions.	• Independent activity where children read, listen to and/or watch two versions of 'The Three Billy Goats Gruff', compare them and express their preferences. • Children's completed photocopiable pages.	**Reading AF6** • Some awareness that writers have viewpoints and purposes. • Simple statements about likes and dislikes in reading, sometimes with reasons.	**Reading AF6** • Comments identify main purpose. • Express personal response but with little awareness of writer's viewpoint or effect on reader.	• I can explore a different version of a story. • I can say which version of a story I like best.
Phase ⑤ activity page 51				
Three Billy Goats Gruff – a play Children can say what a playscript is for and can identify some ways in which it differs from a story text.	• Group activity where children read a playscript and work out their own role play performance using stick puppets. • Group discussion and planning of the performance. • Children's oral feedback and self/peer evaluations.	**Reading AF6** • Some awareness that writers have viewpoints and purposes. • Simple statements about likes and dislikes in reading, sometimes with reasons.	**Reading AF6** • Comments identify main purpose. • Express personal response but with little awareness of writer's viewpoint or effect on reader.	• I can compare a book and a play version of a story. • I can explore a play version of a story. • I can retell a story using puppets.
Phase ⑥ activity page 52				
Writing the story Children can write their own version of a traditional story, using a series of complete sentences organised into chronological order.	• Independent and paired activity where children plan and write their own version of a traditional story. • Children's completed story plans, written stories and peer evaluations.	**Reading AF1** • Range of key words read on sight. • Unfamiliar words decoded using appropriate strategies. • Some fluency and expression. **Writing AF1** • Mostly relevant ideas and content, sometimes repetitive or sparse. • Some apt word choices create interest. • Brief comments, questions about events or actions suggest viewpoint.	**Reading AF1** Range of strategies used mostly effectively to read with fluency, understanding and expression. **Writing AF1** • Some appropriate ideas and content included. • Some attempt to elaborate on basic information or events. • Attempt to adopt viewpoint, though often not maintained or inconsistent.	• I can retell a traditional story in my own words. • I can write a story plan. • I can write my own version of a traditional story.

NARRATIVE

Phase ① Goldilocks and the Three Bears

Learning outcome
Children can identify the main events in traditional tales, sequencing them in chronological order.

Success criteria
- I can retell a traditional tale.
- I can retell a traditional tale by sorting jumbled sentences.

Setting the context
This assessment should be carried out once the children have read and explored several fairy tales and traditional stories in shared and guided reading. They should have compared typical characters, settings and events and described what took place at the beginning, middle and end of the stories. Arrange the children into pairs of similar ability. Provide them with the photocopiable page 'Jumbled sentences', challenging them to cut out and group the sentences under three headings. Invite the children to use the sentences to retell the story to their partner. Encourage them to use sequencing words in their retelling.

Assessment opportunity
Provide the children working at level 1 with version 1 of the photocopiable page, which includes highlighted sequencing words. Children at levels 2–3 should be encouraged to use sequencing words of their own on version 2. Alternatively, the children can complete the interactive activity 'Goldilocks and the Three Bears'. Observe pairs as they sequence the sentences and make notes of their contributions against the class list. Invite pairs of children to retell the story when they have re-ordered the sentences. Invite the others to listen for any differences in the chosen order.

Assessment evidence
At level 1, the children should be able to find the beginning and ending of the story. Children working at level 2 should use simple sequencing words in their retelling such as 'next' and 'then'. At levels 2–3, the children will use more adventurous sequencing words such as 'while', 'later' and 'afterwards'. Use notes made against the class list and the completed photocopiable page to provide evidence against Reading AF2.

Next steps
Support: During guided reading sessions, ask questions to help the children identify the basic story elements such as: *Who was the story about? Where did it take place? How did it start? What happened in the middle of the story? How did it end?*
Extension: Invite the children to use the summarised story on the photocopiable page as a basis for retelling a fuller version to a partner.

Key aspects of learning
Social skills: Children will learn about taking turns, listening to others and trying to reach agreement as they work together in a group.
Communication: Children will develop their ability to speak before an audience as they tell stories for a group.
Evaluation: Children will listen to one another's oral and written stories and give feedback about specific aspects. They will have the chance to judge their own work and decide on areas that they would like to improve.

NARRATIVE

Phase ② Story props

Learning outcome
Children can retell a traditional familiar story in chronological order using story language.

Success criteria
- I can compare traditional tales.
- I can use puppets and props to retell a story.

Setting the context
This assessment should be undertaken once the children have explored and compared several fairy tales and traditional stories. They should have had the chance to identify characters, traditional story language, stock characters and endings. Arrange the children into groups and provide them with puppets and props that could be used when retelling several different stories. Cut out copies of the prop cards from the photocopiable page 'Story props' so there are enough sets for all of the children. Explain that they can choose any number of the prop cards to help them retell a favourite story. Explain that some of the images may be used for more than one story, and more than one may be used for a single story. Invite the children to choose images from the set and any other props they might need, and use these to retell a story to the other members of their group.

Assessment opportunity
This activity provides the opportunity to assess the children's recall of familiar stories and to observe how well they can use traditional story language in retelling a story to the group. A supporting adult can work with groups at level 1. After each child's retelling, encourage the other members of the group to give feedback, using a checklist of criteria if necessary.

Assessment evidence
At level 1, the children will use simple connectives such as 'and', 'then' and 'but'. They may use a clear opening, such as 'once upon a time' and may finish their story abruptly. For example, 'the end'. At levels 2-3, the children will incorporate more traditional story language, such as 'and they lived happily ever after'. They will also use more varied vocabulary to sequence the story. Use the children's oral responses, group feedback and notes made against the class list to provide evidence against Writing AF7.

Next steps
Support: Encourage the children to practise retelling their favourite stories to soft toys or dolls.
Extension: Invite the children to retell their story to a recording device, listen back to it and then consider ways they could improve it.

Key aspects of learning
Social skills: Children will learn about taking turns, listening to others and trying to reach agreement as they work together in a group.
Communication: Children will develop their ability to speak before an audience as they tell stories for a group.
Evaluation: Children will listen to one another's oral and written stories and give feedback about specific aspects. They will have the chance to judge their own work and decide on areas that they would like to improve.

Phase ③ Characters

Learning outcomes
● Children can discuss the appearance, behaviour, characteristics and goals of characters.
● Children can write a profile of a character using visual and written text.

Success criteria
● I can describe the characters in a traditional story.
● I can write a character profile.

Setting the context
Prior to this assessment, the children should have had the opportunity to explore characters in familiar stories, commenting on their appearance and behaviour. They should also be aware of how different characters use dialogue, and that most traditional stories have a good and a bad character. Work together with the children to make a class list of all the good and bad characters that they can remember from the stories you have been reading.

Assessment opportunity
Ask the children to choose a pair of contrasting characters from the list (for example, Little Red Riding Hood and The Big Bad Wolf). Provide them with a copy of the photocopiable page 'Character profile'. Children at level 1 should use version 1 of the photocopiable page, choosing only one character to describe. Ask them to draw a picture of their chosen character and then describe him/her using key words and phrases. Children at levels 2–3 should use version 2 of the photocopiable page. Ask them to describe both a good and bad character using key words and phrases. When the children have completed their character profiles, invite them to swap pages with a partner. Challenge them to work out, from the drawings and/or descriptions, who the characters are and what story they belong to. Invite them to feed back how easy or difficult it was to guess correctly.

Assessment evidence
At level 1, the children will use simple captions and key words to describe a character's appearance, behaviour and language. They should be able to recall some phrases from the original story. At levels 2–3, the children will use full sentences to describe their characters and will incorporate references from the story. Use the children's completed photocopiable pages and partner feedback as evidence against Reading AF2.

Next steps
Support: During guided reading sessions, encourage the children to describe their opinions of characters from traditional stories and fairy tales, and give reasons based on evidence from the text.
Extension: Encourage pairs to use their character profiles to perform a short role play, involving two characters from the same story.

Key aspects of learning
Creative thinking: Children will respond imaginatively to character descriptions, exploring motives and behaviour through role play.
Empathy: Children will consider the thoughts, feelings and actions of characters in stories.

NARRATIVE

Phase ④ The Three Billy Goats Gruff

Learning outcome
Children can discuss how narratives on audio tape or video are presented and express an opinion about the different versions.

Success criteria
● I can explore a different version of a story.
● I can say which version of a story I like best.

Setting the context
Prior to this assessment, the children should have had the opportunity to explore different versions of a familiar traditional story, including visual, audio and playscript formats. They should have had opportunities to join in with repeated words and phrases during shared reading and identified who the characters are, what the setting is and the main events. Share a story book version of *The Three Billy Goats Gruff* with the children. Then play an audio version and/or a visual version of the story to them.

Assessment opportunity
Provide the children with copies of the photocopiable page 'The Three Billy Goats Gruff' (version 1 and 2) and invite them to record their impressions of the different versions by filling in the boxes. At level 1, the children should work in a group with a supporting adult. When the children have completed their photocopiable pages, invite them to describe how the stories were the same or different, which one they preferred and to give a reason. Make notes of their responses against the class list.

Assessment evidence
At level 1, the children should recognise that the characters, events and settings are the same in all versions. At levels 2–3, the children will be able to describe similarities and differences. For example, repeated phrases, differences in dialogue and so on. Make notes against the class list and use the completed photocopiable pages to provide evidence against Reading AF6.

Next steps
Support: Re-read the story book version to the children. Afterwards, share a visual or audio version of the story, pausing it to compare the beginning, middle and ending.
Extension: Invite the children to role play the story in small groups and compare how their own version is the same or different.

Key aspects of learning
Reasoning: Children will have opportunities to compare different versions of stories, to express their opinions and make judgements about which they prefer.
Creative thinking: Children will respond imaginatively to character descriptions, exploring motives and behaviour through role play.
Empathy: Children will consider the thoughts, feelings and actions of characters in stories.

■ SCHOLASTIC

Phase ⑤ Three Billy Goats Gruff – a play

Learning outcome
Children can perform a simple playscript and can identify some ways in which a playscript differs from a story text.

Success criteria
- I can compare a book and a play version of a story.
- I can explore a play version of a story.
- I can retell a story using puppets.

Setting the context
Before performing this assessment, children should have compared different versions of a story, and explored a play version of the same story in shared and guided reading sessions and through role play. Begin the session by reading a play together in a small group. For example, *The Three Billy Goats Gruff* by Julia Donaldson. Afterwards, provide the group with stick or finger puppets and invite them to plan a dramatic version of the play to perform to the rest of the class. (Puppet templates are available on the photocopiable page 'Stick puppets'.)

Assessment opportunity
Invite the groups to perform their plays at a suitable time over the next several days. Ask the audience to comment on what was similar and what was different to the version that they read. Also, invite them to say one thing that was good about each performance and one thing that could be improved. After each group has performed its play, make notes based on your observations and the response of the audience. When all the groups have performed, invite them to express their own opinions about their play. Make notes of their responses against the class list.

Assessment evidence
At level 1, the children will repeat key phrases from the playscript in their role play and express their opinions with simple statements of likes and dislikes. At levels 2–3, the children might include dialogue of their own and give reasons for their likes and dislikes. Children's responses will provide evidence against Reading AF6.

Next steps
Support: Provide guided reading groups with other suitable playscripts to read. Encourage them to add dialogue in their own words.
Extension: Ask the children to choose another traditional tale and write it as a playscript.

Key aspects of learning
Reasoning: Children will have opportunities to compare different versions of stories, to express their opinions and make judgements about which they prefer.
Creative thinking: Children will respond imaginatively to character descriptions, exploring motives and behaviour through role play.
Empathy: Children will consider the thoughts, feelings and actions of characters in stories.
Social skills: Children will learn about taking turns, listening to others and trying to reach agreement as they work together in a group.
Evaluation: Children will listen to one another's oral and written stories and give feedback about specific aspects. They will have the chance to judge their own work and decide on areas that they would like to improve.

Phase ⑥ Writing the story

Learning outcome

Children can write their own version of a traditional story, using a series of complete sentences organised into chronological order.

Success criteria
- I can retell a traditional story in my own words.
- I can write a story plan.
- I can write my own version of a traditional story.

Setting the context
Prior to this assessment, the children should have had the opportunity to retell traditional stories and fairy tales using their own words. They should also have explored how to plan a story, showing a clear beginning, middle and ending. Display an enlarged version of the photocopiable page 'The Princess and the Pea' and read the text together.

Assessment opportunity
Invite the children working at level 1 to complete the interactive activity 'The Princess and the Pea' in pairs, by matching the pictures to the sentences. Afterwards, ask them to plan their own version of the story with their partner, using the photocopiable page 'Story plan' (version 1). At levels 2-3, the children can work independently to plan their story on version 2 of the photocopiable page. Afterwards, all children should move on to writing their story, using their notes as a guide. After the children have written their stories, ask them to perform their story to their partner, who should then give feedback. Ask the partners to comment on two things that were done well and one thing that could be improved upon. For those children who planned their stories in pairs, invite them to compare their finished versions with their notes to see how closely they match.

Assessment evidence
At level 1, the children will use some simple description in their story writing. When completing the interactive activity, they will match text to the images by identifying key words that relate to the image. At levels 2-3, the children will use more adventurous vocabulary and include some simple dialogue. Make notes against the class list of children's responses to their partners' stories to provide evidence against Writing AF1. Use the completed interactive activity as evidence against Reading AF1.

Next steps
Support: Remind the children to organise their writing to show a clear beginning, middle and ending.
Extension: Invite the children to rewrite their story as a playscript that includes a narrator.

Key aspects of learning
Empathy: Children will consider the thoughts, feelings and actions of characters in stories.
Social skills: Children will learn about taking turns, listening to others and trying to reach agreement as they work together in a group.
Evaluation: Children will listen to one another's oral and written stories and give feedback about specific aspects. They will have the chance to judge their own work and decide on areas that they would like to improve.

Periodic assessment

Reading

Learning outcomes
- Children can identify the main events in traditional tales, sequencing them in chronological order.
- Children can say what a playscript is for and can identify some ways in which it differs from a story text.

Success criteria
- I can retell a familiar traditional tale.
- I can compare a book and play version of a story.

Setting the context
This assessment should be carried out once the children have completed the work from this unit. Ensure the children have had experience of reading and exploring different traditional stories and fairy tales, in book and play versions, during shared and guided reading. Review the work that has been done during the course of this unit and discuss the children's achievements with them. Ask them what they found easy to accomplish and what was difficult. Make notes of their responses against the class list.

Assessment opportunity
Invite the children to choose one of the stories from the unit and its corresponding playscript. Ask them to give an oral description, to their group or class, of how the versions are similar and different. Encourage them to support their points with evidence from the text.

Assessment evidence
At levels 2–3, the children's responses will contain basic, straightforward information recalled from the story, with references to the beginning, middle and ending. They may include comments on the use of dialogue and narrator in plays and the different layouts. Draw out the responses of children working at level 1 by questioning. For example, *How does the play begin? How is that different from the story?* Use children's oral self-assessments and notes against the class list to provide evidence against Reading AF2 and AF4.

NARRATIVE

Periodic assessment

Writing

Learning outcomes
- Children can write a profile of a character using visual and written text.
- Children can write their own version of a traditional story, using a series of complete sentences organised into chronological order.

Success criteria
- I can write a character profile.
- I can retell a traditional story in my own words.
- I can write my own version of a traditional story.

Setting the context
Collect the work that has been completed during the course of this unit and go through each individual child's achievements with them. Ask them to suggest what they found difficult about the writing in the unit and what they found easy to accomplish. Make notes of their responses against the class list.

Assessment opportunity
Ask the children to choose the piece of writing they struggled with the most. Look through it together and talk about what is needed to improve it, taking into account what they have learned during the whole unit. Identify vocabulary choices that could be improved upon, and words used to describe a character or sequence a story. Encourage them to edit and add to their work, in order to polish it. When the children have completed their improvements, ask them to swap their written work with a partner. Invite the partners to describe why and how it has been improved.

Assessment evidence
At level 1, the children may identify simple vocabulary choices that could be improved. For example, using 'terrible' instead of 'bad'. At levels 2–3, the children may improve their choices of adjectives and punctuation. The children's oral responses of their own achievements and their partner's evaluations can be used to provide evidence against Writing AF1 and AF8.

Story props

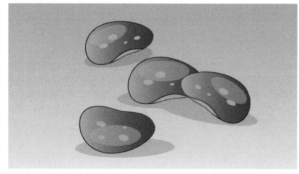

NARRATIVE

Illustrations © 2010, Anna Godwin/The Illustrator Agency.

NARRATIVE

Stick puppets

Illustrations © 2010, Anna Godwin / The Illustrator Agency.

Name	Date

Story plan (1)

Beginning

Middle

Ending

Illustrations © 2010, Anna Godwin / The Illustrator Agency.

Red
Amber
Green

I can write a story plan. ☐

NARRATIVE

UNIT 4 Stories about fantasy worlds

Literacy objectives

Speak and listen for a wide range of purposes in different contexts
Strand 4 Drama
- Explore familiar themes and characters through improvisation and role play.

Read for a range of purposes on paper and on screen
Strand 5 Word recognition: decoding (reading) and encoding (spelling)
- Recognise and use alternative ways of pronouncing the graphemes already taught.
- Recognise and use alternative ways of spelling the phonemes already taught.
- Identify the constituent parts of two-syllable and three-syllable words to support the application of phonic knowledge and skills.
- Recognise automatically an increasing number of familiar high frequency words.
- Apply phonic knowledge and skills as the prime approach to reading and spelling unfamiliar words that are not completely decodable.
- Read more challenging texts which can be decoded using their acquired phonic knowledge and skills, along with automatic recognition of high frequency words.
- Read and spell phonically decodable two-syllable and three-syllable words.

Strand 6 Word structure and spelling
- Spell new words using phonics as the prime approach.
- Segment sounds into their constituent phonemes in order to spell them correctly.
- Recognise and use alternative ways of spelling the graphemes already taught.
- Use knowledge of common inflections in spelling, such as plurals, *-ly*, *-er.*
- Read and spell phonically decodable two-syllable and three-syllable words.

Strand 7 Understanding and interpreting texts
- Use syntax and context when reading for meaning.
- Recognise the main elements that shape different texts.

Strand 9 Creating and shaping texts
- Use key features of narrative in their own writing.
- Create short simple texts on paper and screen that combine words with images (and sounds).

Strand 11 Sentence structure and punctuation
- Compose and write simple sentences independently to communicate meaning.
- Use capital letters and full stops when punctuating simple sentences.

Strand 12 Presentation
- Use the space bar and keyboard to type their name and simple texts.

Key aspects of learning

Problem solving
- Children will identify problems and resolutions for a main character, applying their prior experience of adventure narratives to consider a range of possible solutions.

Creative thinking
- Children will generate imaginative ideas in response to visual stimuli and make connections through play.

SCHOLASTIC

Key aspects of learning (continued)

Reasoning
● Children will predict events in a text, expressing and justifying their opinions based on evidence from the text and prior experience.
Empathy
● Children will consider the thoughts, feelings and actions of characters in stories.
Communication
● Children will develop their ability to discuss as they work collaboratively in paired, group and whole-class contexts. They will communicate outcomes orally, in writing and through ICT.

Assessment focuses

Reading
AF3 *(deduce, infer or interpret information, events or ideas from texts).*

Writing
AF1 *(write imaginative, interesting and thoughtful texts).*
AF3 *(organise and present whole texts effectively, sequencing and structuring information, ideas and events).*
AF5 *(vary sentences for clarity, purpose and effect).*
AF6 *(write with technical accuracy of syntax and punctuation in phrases, clauses and sentences).*

Speaking and listening
Drama (improvise and sustain roles).

Resources

Phase 1 activities
Photocopiable page, 'Objects and characters' (versions 1 and 2)
Interactive activity, 'Identifying settings'
Photocopiable page, 'Fantasy island'
Phase 2 activities
Photocopiable page, 'Fantasy role-play plan'
Phase 3 activities
Photocopiable page, 'Story planner'
Photocopiable page, 'What is happening?' (versions 1 and 2)
Interactive activity, 'Missing punctuation'
Image, 'The search for the magic ruby'
Photocopiable page, 'Undersea adventure'
Periodic assessment
Photocopiable page, 'Narrative 4 Reading assessment'

Unit 4 □ Stories about fantasy worlds

Learning outcomes	Assessment opportunity and evidence	Assessment focuses (AFs)		Success criteria
		Level 1		
Phase ① activities pages 63-64				
Fantasy setting Children can predict possible events in a narrative based on their experience of other texts.	● Independent and paired activity where children compare the objects and characters in fairy tale settings with those in fantasy settings. ● Paired discussion of the story settings. ● Children's completed photocopiable pages and interactive activity.	**Reading AF3** ● Reasonable inference at a basic level. ● Comments/questions about meaning of parts of text.		● I can compare fantasy worlds. ● I can explore pictures of fantasy worlds. ● I can recognise objects from fantasy worlds.
Fantasy island Children can predict possible events in a narrative based on their experience of other texts.	● Paired activity where children explore an image of a fantasy island and describe to a partner what might happen in a story set on this island. ● Paired discussion of the image and sharing of story ideas. ● Children's oral responses and annotated photocopiable pages.	**Writing AF1** ● Basic information and ideas conveyed through appropriate word choice. ● Some descriptive language.		● I can make up a story in a fantasy setting. ● I can explore what might happen to a character in a fantasy setting.
Phase ② activity page 65				
Fantasy role play Children can orally tell an adventure narrative during role play with the events organised sequentially into problems and resolution.	● Paired activity where children plan a fantasy role play by drawing the beginning, middle and ending of their story. They then perform their role play to other groups. ● Paired discussion and planning of the role play. ● Children's completed photocopiable, role play performance and peer feedback.	**Writing AF3** ● Some formulaic phrases indicate start/end of text. ● Events/ideas sometimes in appropriate order.		● I can choose the setting and characters for an adventure story. ● I can introduce a problem and a resolution. ● I can retell my story orally.
Phase ③ activities pages 66-67				
A fantasy walk Children can compose complete sentences correctly demarcated by capital letters and full stops.	● Independent activity where children role play taking a walk through a fantasy environment and record their walk using simple sentences. The interactive activity and photocopiable pages provide further practice at composing complete sentences. ● Individual role play performances to the class or group. ● Children's completed photocopiable pages and interactive activity.	**Writing AF5** ● Reliance on simple phrases and clauses. ● Some sentence-like structures formed by chaining clauses together. **Writing AF6** ● Mostly grammatically accurate clauses. ● Some awareness of use of full stops and capital letters.		● I can explore a fantasy setting through role play. ● I can plan a story with a beginning, middle and end. ● I can write sentences that make sense and have correct punctuation.

Unit 4 ☐ Stories about fantasy worlds

Learning outcomes	Assessment opportunity and evidence	Assessment focuses (AFs)	Success criteria
		Level 1	
Problems and resolutions Children can write a short story with the events organised sequentially into problem and resolution.	• Supported group activity where children compose sentences that convey more information about an image. • Group discussion of the story image. • Children's oral responses and completed photocopiable.	**Writing AF1** • Basic information and ideas conveyed through appropriate word choice. • Some descriptive language.	• I can identify a problem and resolution for a character. • I can write sentences that make sense and have correct punctuation.

Learning outcomes	Assessment opportunity and evidence	Assessment focuses (AFs)		Success criteria
		Level 2	**Level 3**	

Phase ① activities pages 63-64

Learning outcomes	Assessment opportunity and evidence	Level 2	Level 3	Success criteria
Fantasy setting Children can predict possible events in a narrative based on their experience of other texts.	• Independent and paired activity where children compare the objects and characters in fairy tale settings with those in fantasy settings. • Paired discussion of the story settings. • Children's completed photocopiable pages and interactive activity.	**Reading AF3** • Simple, plausible inference about events and information, using evidence form text. • Comments based on textual clues, sometimes misunderstood.	**Reading AF3** • Straightforward inference based on a single point of reference in the text. • Responses to text show meaning established at a literal level.	• I can compare fantasy worlds. • I can explore pictures of fantasy worlds. • I can recognise objects from fantasy worlds.
Fantasy island Children can predict possible events in a narrative based on their experience of other texts.	• Paired activity where children explore an image of a fantasy island and describe to a partner what might happen in a story set on this island. • Paired discussion of the image and sharing of story ideas. • Children's oral responses and annotated photocopiable pages.	**Writing AF1** • Mostly relevant ideas and content, sometimes repetitive or sparse. • Some apt word choices create interest. • Brief comments, questions about events or actions suggest viewpoint.	**Writing AF1** • Some appropriate ideas and content included. • Some attempt to elaborate on basic information or events. • Attempt to adopt viewpoint, though often not maintained or inconsistent.	• I can make up a story in a fantasy setting. • I can explore what might happen to a character in a fantasy setting.

Phase ② activity page 65

Learning outcomes	Assessment opportunity and evidence	Level 2	Level 3	Success criteria
Fantasy role play Children can orally tell an adventure narrative during role play with the events organised sequentially into problems and resolution.	• Paired activity where children plan a fantasy role play using images and written notes. They then perform their role play to other groups. • Paired discussion and planning of the role play. • Children's completed photocopiable, role play performance and peer feedback.	**Writing AF3** • Some basic sequencing of ideas or material. • Openings and/or closings sometimes signalled.	**Writing AF3** • Some attempt to organise ideas with related points placed next to each other. • Openings and closings usually signalled. • Some attempt to sequence ideas or material logically.	• I can choose the setting and characters for an adventure story. • I can introduce a problem and a resolution. • I can retell my story orally.

Unit 4 📖 Stories about fantasy worlds

Learning outcomes	Assessment opportunity and evidence	Assessment focuses (AFs)		Success criteria
		Level 2	Level 3	
Phase ③ activities pages 66-67				
A fantasy walk Children can compose complete sentences correctly demarcated by capital letters and full stops.	• Independent activity where children role play taking a walk through a fantasy environment and record their walk using simple sentences. The interactive activity and photocopiable pages provide further practice at composing complete sentences. • Individual role play performances to the class or group. • Children's completed photocopiable pages and interactive activity.	**Writing AF5** • Some variation in sentence openings. • Mainly simple sentences with *and* used to connect clauses. • Past and present tense generally consistent. **Writing AF6** • Clause structure mostly grammatically correct. • Sentence demarcation with capital letters and full stops usually accurate. • Some accurate use of question and exclamation marks, and commas in lists.	**Writing AF5** • Reliance mainly on simply structured sentences, variation with support. • *and, but, so* are the most common connectives, subordination occasionally. • Some limited variation in use of tense and verb forms, not always secure. **Writing AF6** • Straightforward sentences usually demarcated accurately with full stops, capital letters, question and exclamation marks. • Some, limited, use of speech punctuation. • Comma splicing evident, particularly in narrative.	• I can explore a fantasy setting through role play. • I can plan a story with a beginning, middle and end. • I can write sentences that make sense and have correct punctuation.
Problems and resolutions Children can write a short story with the events organised sequentially into problem and resolution.	• Paired activity where children compose sentences that convey more information about an image. • Paired discussion of the story image. • Children's oral responses and completed photocopiable.	**Writing AF1** • Mostly relevant ideas and content, sometimes repetitive or sparse. • Some apt word choices create interest. • Brief comments, questions about events or actions suggest viewpoint.	**Writing AF1** • Some appropriate ideas and content included. • Some attempt to elaborate on basic information or events. • Attempt to adopt viewpoint, though often not maintained or inconsistent.	• I can identify a problem and resolution for a character. • I can write sentences that make sense and have correct punctuation.

Phase ① Fantasy setting

Learning outcome
Children can predict possible events in a narrative based on their experience of other texts.

Success criteria
- I can compare fantasy worlds.
- I can explore pictures of fantasy worlds.
- I can recognise objects from fantasy worlds.

Setting the context
This assessment should be carried out once the children have compared and explored several different settings from fairy tales and fantasy stories in shared and guided reading. They should have explored the sorts of objects and characters found in fantasy settings and compared them with the characters and objects found in fairy tales and stories with familiar settings. Provide the children with the photocopiable page 'Objects and characters' (versions 1 and 2) and ask them to look closely at the pictures featured.

Assessment opportunity
Invite the children to draw a circle around any objects they find in the pictures that indicate what sort of stories would take place in these settings. Tell them to use blue circles for fantasy stories and red circles for fairy stories. Encourage the children at levels 2–3 to write labels for the objects they find. For the children who may need extra practice at comparing settings, provide them with the interactive activity 'Identifying settings'. When the children have completed the photocopiable page and/or the interactive activity, invite them to look at the images again. Ask them to consider the types of characters they may meet in each of the settings. What might happen next? Encourage them to share their ideas with you or a talk partner.

Assessment evidence
At level 1, the children should be able to use blue to circle objects in the first picture and red for the second picture on version 1 of the photocopiable page. They should also be able to describe the scenes orally and understand that the first image is the setting for an underwater adventure. At levels 2–3, the children will be able to circle and label the objects correctly on version 2 of the photocopiable page. Use the children's oral responses, the completed photocopiable pages and interactive activity to provide evidence against Reading AF3.

Next steps
Support: During guided reading sessions, encourage the children to explore illustrations to identify objects and other features that show where the story is set.
Extension: Invite the children to choose a setting from the photocopiable page and make up a story to tell their partner.

Key aspects of learning
Creative thinking: Children will generate imaginative ideas in response to visual stimuli and make connections through play.
Reasoning: Children will predict events in a text, expressing and justifying their opinions based on evidence from the text and prior experience.

NARRATIVE

Phase ① Fantasy island

Learning outcome
Children can predict possible events in a narrative based on their experience of other texts.

Success criteria
● I can make up a story in a fantasy setting.
● I can explore what might happen to a character in a fantasy setting.

Setting the context
The children should have already completed the previous activity and had the opportunity to explore fantasy settings of their own invention through role play and drawing. Display a copy of the photocopiable page 'Fantasy island'. Discuss the various features of the island, as you trace a journey around the island with your finger. When you stop at each of the features, talk about the types of things that you might see or experience at each location. Write these as key words, adding them to the image. Explore some alternative journeys, starting and finishing at a different location.

Assessment opportunity
In pairs, provide the children with their own copies of the photocopiable page. Invite them to explore the map and then make up a story based on the island to share with their partner. Ask them to write and/or draw the events and characters on their page, and add any fantasy objects that might be found in the different locations onto the map. When the children have shared their ideas with a partner, display the island image again and ask individual children to describe their ideas for a fantasy story to the others in the group or class. Make notes of their contributions against the class list.

Assessment evidence
At level 1, the children will use simple language to describe their story with little elaboration and little use of descriptive language. For example, 'And then I saw a cave. There was a monster in it'. At levels 2–3, the children will use more descriptive vocabulary and include vocabulary to sequence the story. For example, 'When I came near to the cave, I heard a strange sound coming from it'. Use the children's oral responses, annotated photocopiable pages and notes made against the class list to provide evidence against Writing AF1.

Next steps
Support: In guided writing, encourage the children to add extra description to the map by noting adjectives and adverbs.
Extension: Invite the children to use a writing frame and make notes to plan an adventure on the fantasy island.

Key aspects of learning
Problem solving: Children will identify problems and resolutions for a main character, applying their prior experience of adventure narratives to consider a range of possible solutions.
Creative thinking: Children will generate imaginative ideas in response to visual stimuli and make connections through play.
Communication: Children will develop their ability to discuss as they work collaboratively in paired, group and whole-class contexts. They will communicate outcomes orally, in writing and through ICT.

Phase ② Fantasy role play

Learning outcome
Children can orally tell an adventure narrative during role play with the events organised sequentially into problem and resolution.

Success criteria
● I can choose the setting and characters for an adventure story.
● I can introduce a problem and a resolution.
● I can retell my story orally.

Setting the context
Prior to this assessment, the children should have had an opportunity to plan a whole-class narrative in role play sessions, and generated ideas for settings and characters using photographs. They should have acted out the whole-class story together and used this experience to plan and role play their own narrative adventure. Remind the children about the whole-class narrative and retell it. Display the photocopiable page 'Fantasy island' from the previous activity and explain to the children that they will be re-using it to create a new role play adventure.

Assessment opportunity
In pairs, provide the children with individual copies of the photocopiable page 'Fantasy role-play plan' and return their story ideas from the previous session. Using these ideas, challenge the children to work together to make a new plan for an adventure story set on the island, that they can role play for the class. The children working at level 1 can draw the beginning, middle and ending of their story, adding simple notes or key words afterwards. At levels 2–3, the children can combine pictures with more extensive written notes to help them plan. When the children have had sufficient time to plan their stories, invite pairs to perform their role play for others in the class or group.

Assessment evidence
At level 1, the children will draw the beginning, middle and ending using one image for each part. Some may add key words to describe who does what in the role play. At levels 2–3, the children will draw and write more than one sentence to describe the problem and resolution. Use the children's completed photocopiable pages, role plays and peer feedback as evidence against Writing AF3.

Next steps
Support: Help the children to plan problems and resolutions during guided writing sessions by providing them with several simple problems and asking them to suggest how the problems could be solved.
Extension: Encourage the children to work in groups of three or four to add extra characters and detail to their role plays.

Key aspects of learning
Problem solving: Children will identify problems and resolutions for a main character, applying their prior experience of adventure narratives to consider a range of possible solutions.
Creative thinking: Children will generate imaginative ideas in response to visual stimuli and make connections through play.
Communication: Children will develop their ability to discuss as they work collaboratively in paired, group and whole-class contexts. They will communicate outcomes orally, in writing and through ICT.

NARRATIVE

Phase ③ A fantasy walk

Success criteria
- I can explore a fantasy setting through role play.
- I can plan a story with a beginning, middle and end.
- I can write sentences that make sense and have correct punctuation.

Setting the context
This assessment should be undertaken once the children have explored settings, problems and resolutions in role play sessions. They should also have had the opportunity to learn about the writing process and used complete sentences with punctuation in modelled writing sessions. Explain to the children that they are going to role play walking through their fantasy setting and, while doing so, say aloud what they want to happen using complete sentences. Model how to do this by demonstrating. For example, *Peter arrives at the white tower. He sees that the door is guarded by a fierce dog. He needs to get in, so he...* and so on.

Assessment opportunity
Invite the children to act out and speak their story. Immediately afterwards, ask them to record their sentences on the photocopiable page 'Story planner'. Once this is done, the children can move onto the photocopiable page 'What is happening?' (versions 1 and 2) and the interactive activity 'Missing punctuation'. The interactive activity will provide an opportunity to assess how well the children recognise sentences where the correct punctuation is missing.

Assessment evidence
At level 1, the children will mostly use simple phrases or clauses and joining words such as 'and' and 'then'. At levels 2–3, the children will use simple and some compound sentences, including occasional question marks and exclamation marks. Make notes against the class list of children's oral responses and use the completed photocopiable activities to provide evidence against Writing AF5 and AF6.

Next steps
Support: For children who have difficulty in varying their sentence forms, create sentences with them in guided writing to demonstrate how to vary the opening of a sentence.
Extension: Invite the children to use the sentences on the story planner to begin to write their own narratives.

Key aspects of learning
Problem solving: Children will identify problems and resolutions for a main character, applying their prior experience of adventure narratives to consider a range of possible solutions.
Creative thinking: Children will generate imaginative ideas in response to visual stimuli and make connections through play.
Communication: Children will develop their ability to discuss as they work collaboratively in paired, group and whole-class contexts. They will communicate outcomes orally, in writing and through ICT.

Phase ③ Problems and resolutions

Learning outcome
Children can write a short story with the events organised sequentially into problem and resolution.

Success criteria
- I can identify a problem and resolution for a character.
- I can write sentences that make sense and have correct punctuation.

Setting the context
Prior to this assessment, the children should have worked on their own fantasy stories and explored the use of images to convey information to readers. Display the image 'The search for the magic ruby'. Invite the children to describe the information that is contained in the image and discuss what text might be needed to elaborate on the story. Model adding a sentence to the image.

Assessment opportunity
Provide the children with their own copies of the photocopiable page 'Undersea adventure'. Explain that you want them to write one or two sentences that will give additional information about the problem faced by the main character, that isn't shown in the image. They should also include a resolution to the problem. Encourage them to share their ideas with a partner before writing. The children working at level 1 should work in a supported group. When they have written their sentences, ask individual children to describe what they think the picture is telling them about the story, and then to read their sentences aloud. During a plenary session, discuss the differences and similarities in the children's ideas and how well they solved the problems. Make notes of their responses against the class list.

Assessment evidence
At level 1, the children will write one or two simple sentences, mostly based on what they can see in the picture. At levels 2-3, the children may include a sentence describing what happened before the picture and a simple resolution. Use the children's completed photocopiable pages and notes against the class list to provide evidence against Writing AF1.

Next steps
Support: Encourage the children to identify problems and resolutions in guided reading sessions.
Extension: Encourage the children to use ICT to find images for stories and add sentences using a keyboard.

Key aspects of learning
Problem solving: Children will identify problems and resolutions for a main character, applying their prior experience of adventure narratives to consider a range of possible solutions.
Creative thinking: Children will generate imaginative ideas in response to visual stimuli and make connections through play.
Reasoning: Children will predict events in a text, expressing and justifying their opinions based on evidence from the text and prior experience.
Empathy: Children will consider the thoughts, feelings and actions of characters in stories.
Communication: Children will develop their ability to discuss as they work collaboratively in paired, group and whole-class contexts. They will communicate outcomes orally, in writing and through ICT.

NARRATIVE

Periodic assessment

Reading

Learning outcomes
● Children can predict possible events in a narrative based on their experience of other texts.
● Children can orally tell an adventure narrative during role play with the events organised sequentially into problem and resolution.

Success criteria
● I can compare fantasy worlds.
● I can explore images in fantasy worlds.
● I can explore features of a fantasy story.

Setting the context
Collect the work that has been completed during the course of this unit and discuss, with each child, their individual achievements. Ask them what they found easy to accomplish and what was difficult. Make notes of their responses against the class list.

Assessment opportunity
Invite the children to choose one of the stories read during the course of the unit and complete the photocopiable page 'Narrative 4 Reading assessment'. This assessment provides an opportunity to evaluate the children's understanding of the features of fantasy stories and the importance of understanding the problem and how it is resolved. It also provides an opportunity to compare your own assessments with the children's self-evaluations.

Assessment evidence
At level 1, the children may need prompting to recall their story. For example, *How does the story begin? What problem does the main character face? How does he or she solve it?* At levels 2–3, the children's responses will contain basic, straightforward information recalled from the story with references to the beginning, middle and ending. Use the children's oral self-assessments and notes against the class list to provide evidence against Reading AF2 and AF4.

Periodic assessment

Writing

Learning outcomes
- Children can compose complete sentences correctly demarcated by capital letters and full stops.
- Children can write a short story with the events organised sequentially into problem and resolution.

Success criteria
- I can plan a story with a beginning, middle and end.
- I can write sentences that make sense and have correct punctuation.
- I can write a story with a beginning, middle and end.

Setting the context
Review the children's written work over the course of this unit. Invite them to explain what they found easy and what they found difficult about the writing. Make notes of their responses against the class list.

Assessment opportunity
Ask the children to choose a piece of writing from the beginning of the unit. Look through it together and talk about what is needed to improve it, taking into account what they have learned during the whole unit. Identify the beginning, middle and ending; problem and resolution. Discuss what could be improved upon. Encourage them to add anything needed to polish the piece. When the children have completed their improvements, ask them to swap their writing with a partner. Invite the partners to describe how and why the writing has been improved.

Assessment evidence
At level 1, the children may identify simple vocabulary choices or uses of punctuation that have been worked on. At levels 2–3, the children may comment on the choice of problem or the way it has been resolved. The children's oral responses and their partners' evaluations can be used to provide evidence against Writing AF1.

NARRATIVE

Name   Date

Objects and characters (1)

◢ Find the objects and characters that show what sort of story these pictures come from.

◢ Circle the objects and characters from fantasy stories in blue.

◢ Circle the objects and characters from fairy stories in red.

Red / Amber / Green

I can compare fantasy worlds. ☐

I can explore pictures of fantasy worlds. ☐

I can recognise objects from fantasy worlds. ☐

Illustrations © 2010, Anna Godwin/The Illustrator Agency.

Name	Date

What is happening? (1)

◖ Look at the pictures and finish the sentences about what is happening.

Mark was playing football near the river when _____ _____ _____

A lady came to help. Mark _____ _____ _____

She ran along the river bank to _____ _____ _____

The lady _____ _____ _____ _____

Red
Amber
Green

I can write sentences that make sense and have correct punctuation. ☐

Illustrations © 2010, Anna Godwin/The Illustrator Agency.

NARRATIVE

Name	Date

Undersea adventure

◼ What is the problem and resolution? Write sentences to tell readers more about the story.

_____

_____

_____

_____

_____

_____

Red	◯	I can identify a problem and resolution for a character. ☐
Amber	◯	I can write sentences that make sense and have correct
Green	◯	punctuation. ☐

Illustration © 2010, Anna Godwin/The Illustrator Agency.

Name

Date

NARRATIVE

Narrative 4 Reading assessment

Book review

Title:
Setting:
Main character:
What happens in the story?
How is the problem solved?
Colour in the stars to rate this story: ☆☆☆☆☆
I like this story because:

Red	I can compare fantasy worlds. ☐
Amber	I can explore images in fantasy worlds. ☐
Green	I can explore features of a fantasy story. ☐

NON-FICTION
UNIT 1 Labels, lists and captions

Literacy objectives

Speak and listen for a wide range of purposes in different contexts

Strand 1 Speaking
- Tell stories and describe incidents from their own experience in an audible voice.

Strand 2 Listening and responding
- Listen with sustained concentration, building new stores of words in different contexts.
- Listen to and follow instructions accurately, asking for help and clarification if necessary.

Strand 3 Group discussion and interaction
- Take turns to speak, listen to each others' suggestions and talk about what they are going to do.
- Ask and answer questions, make relevant contributions, offer suggestions and take turns.

Read and write for a range of purposes on paper and on screen

Strand 5 Word recognition: decoding (reading) and encoding (spelling)
- Recognise and use alternative ways of pronouncing the graphemes already taught.
- Recognise and use alternative ways of spelling the phonemes already taught.
- Identify the constituent parts of two-syllable and three-syllable words to support the application of phonic knowledge and skills.
- Recognise automatically an increasing number of familiar high frequency words.
- Apply phonic knowledge and skills as the prime approach to reading and spelling unfamiliar words that are not completely decodable.
- Read more challenging texts which can be decoded using their acquired phonic knowledge and skills, along with automatic recognition of high frequency words.
- Read and spell phonically decodable two-syllable and three-syllable words.

Strand 6 Word structure and spelling
- Spell new words using phonics as the prime approach.
- Segment sounds into their constituent phonemes in order to spell them correctly.
- Recognise and use alternative ways of spelling the graphemes already taught.
- Use knowledge of common inflections in spelling such as plurals, -*ly*, -*er*.
- Read and spell phonically decodable two-syllable and three-syllable words.

Strand 7 Understanding and interpreting texts
- Identify the main events and characters in stories, and find specific information in simple texts.
- Explore the effect of patterns of language and repeated words and phrases.

Strand 8 Engaging with and responding to texts
- Distinguish fiction and non-fiction texts and the different purposes for reading them.

Strand 9 Creating and shaping texts
- Independently choose what to write about, plan and follow it through.
- Convey information and ideas in simple non-narrative forms.
- Create short simple texts on paper and screen that combine words with images (and sounds).

Strand 10 Text structure and organisation
- Write chronological and non-chronological texts using simple structures.
- Group written sentences together in chunks of meaning or subject.

Strand 11 Sentence structure and punctuation
- Compose and write simple sentences independently to communicate meaning.
- Use capital letters and full stops when punctuating simple sentences.

Strand 12 Presentation
- Use the space bar and keyboard to type their name and simple texts.

Key aspects of learning

Enquiry
● Children will ask questions arising from work on classroom routines and plan how to present the information effectively.

Reasoning
● Children will explain why certain labels and captions are appropriate.

Communication
● Children will develop their ability to discuss as they work collaboratively in pairs and in a whole-class context. They will communicate outcomes orally, in writing and through ICT if appropriate.

Assessment focuses

Reading
AF4 *(identify and comment on the structure and organisation of texts, including grammatical and presentational features at text level).*

Writing
AF2 *(produce texts which are appropriate to task, reader and purpose).*
AF6 *(write with technical accuracy of syntax and punctuation in phrases, clauses and sentences).*

Speaking and listening
Speaking (speak with clarity, intonation and pace).
Listening and responding (listen to others in class, ask relevant questions and follow instructions).
Group discussion and interaction (make contributions to sustain an activity, offer suggestions and take turns).

Resources

Phase 1 activities
Interactive activity, 'Choose the label'
Phase 2 activities
Photocopiable page, 'Captions'
Phase 3 activities
Photocopiable page, 'Writing captions'
Photocopiable page, 'Caption choices' (versions 1 and 2)

Unit 1 🖳 Labels, lists and captions

Learning outcomes	Assessment opportunity and evidence	Assessment focuses (AFs)	Success criteria
		Level 1	
Phase ① activity page 78			
Labels Children can say what the purposes of lists and labels in the classroom are.	• Paired activity where children complete an interactive activity, matching labels and lists to images, and then identify labels and lists around the classroom. • Paired discussion while matching labels and lists for the interactive activity. • Children's completed interactive activity and oral responses.	**Reading AF4** Some awareness of meaning of simple text features.	• I know what a label is. • I know what a list is.
Phase ② activity page 79			
Captions Children can give a complete sentence as a caption for an object or picture.	• Supported activity where children identify capital letters and full stops on three captioned illustrations and think of a suitable caption for one illustration. • Children's completed photocopiable page and oral responses.	**Reading AF4** Some awareness of meaning of simple text features.	• I can spot capital letters and full stops. • I can think of and say a caption.
Phase ③ activity page 80			
Writing a caption Children write a caption for an object or picture in a complete sentence with a capital letter and full stop.	• Paired activity where children choose the most appropriate captions for an image. They then complete a cut-and-stick activity, matching captions to a choice of pictures. • Whole-class discussion and captioning of the image. • Children's oral responses and completed cut-and-stick activity.	**Writing AF2** Some indication of basic purpose, particular form or awareness of reader. **Writing AF6** • Mostly grammatically accurate clauses. • Some awareness of use of full stops and capital letters.	• I can choose a caption for a picture. • I can write a caption.

Unit 1 📖 Labels, lists and captions

Learning outcomes	Assessment opportunity and evidence	Assessment focuses (AFs)		Success criteria
		Level 2	Level 3	
Phase ① activity page 78				
Labels Children can say what the purposes of lists and labels in the classroom are.	● Paired activity where children complete an interactive activity, matching labels and lists to images, and then identify labels and lists around the classroom. ● Paired discussion while matching labels and lists for the interactive activity. ● Children's completed interactive activity and oral responses.	**Reading AF4** Some awareness of use of features of organisation.	**Reading AF4** A few basic features of organisation at text level identified, with little or no linked comment.	● I know what a label is. ● I know what a list is.
Phase ② activity page 79				
Captions Children can give a complete sentence as a caption for an object or picture.	● Independent activity where children identify capital letters and full stops on three captioned illustrations and think of a suitable caption for one illustration. ● Children's completed photocopiable page and oral responses.	**Reading AF4** Some awareness of use of features of organisation.	**Reading AF4** A few basic features of organisation at text level identified, with little or no linked comment.	● I can spot capital letters and full stops. ● I can think of and say a caption.
Phase ③ activity page 80				
Writing a caption Children write a caption for an object or picture in a complete sentence with a capital letter and full stop.	● Paired activity where children choose the most appropriate captions for an image. They then complete a cut-and-stick activity, matching captions to a choice of pictures. ● Whole-class discussion and captioning of the image. ● Children's oral responses and completed cut-and-stick activity.	**Writing AF2** ● Some basic purpose established. ● Some appropriate features of the given form used. ● Some attempts to adopt appropriate style. **Writing AF6** ● Clause structure mostly grammatically correct. ● Sentence demarcation with capital letters and full stops usually accurate. ● Some accurate use of question and exclamation marks, and commas in lists.	**Writing AF2** ● Purpose established at a general level. ● Main features of selected form sometimes signalled to the reader. ● Some attempts at appropriate style, with attention to reader. **Writing AF6** ● Straightforward sentences usually demarcated with full stops, capital letters, question and exclamation marks. ● Some, limited, use of speech punctuation. ● Comma splicing evident, particularly in narrative.	● I can choose a caption for a picture. ● I can write a caption.

NON-FICTION

Phase ① Labels

Learning outcome
Children can say what the purposes of lists and labels in the classroom are.

Success criteria
- I know what a label is.
- I know what a list is.

Setting the context
Prior to this assessment, the children should have participated in setting up and labelling a classroom display. They should have been introduced to labels and lists and talked about their purposes and uses. They should also have had experience of writing their own labels and lists, such as their names under different headings such as 'dark hair/fair hair', and labels for specific working areas in the classroom. In pairs, give the children the interactive activity 'Choose the label' to complete. Explain that they should look closely at the pictures on the screen and choose a label from the two options provided.

Assessment opportunity
When the children have completed the activity, ask them to tell you how they could tell what the correct labels were. Invite them to look around the classroom and identify places where they can see labels, and places where they can see lists. Make notes of their oral responses against the class list.

Assessment evidence
At level 1, the children will be able to give a simple explanation of the purpose of a label. For example, 'it tells you what something is'. At levels 2–3, the children will be able to give more detail. For example, 'a label tells you one thing about a picture. A list tells you lots of things'. Make notes of their oral responses and use these, together with the completed interactive activity, to provide evidence against Reading AF4.

Next steps
Support: Take opportunities to point out labels in other areas of the school and playground. Read them with the children and encourage them to say why labels have been used.
Extension: Encourage the children to write their own labels for a classroom display.

Key aspects of learning
Enquiry: Children will ask questions arising from work on classroom routines and plan how to present the information effectively.
Reasoning: Children will explain why certain labels and captions are appropriate.
Communication: Children will develop their ability to discuss as they work collaboratively in pairs and in a whole-class context. They will communicate outcomes orally, in writing and through ICT if appropriate.

Phase ② Captions

Learning outcome
Children can give a complete sentence as a caption for an object or picture.

Success criteria
- I can spot capital letters and full stops.
- I can think of and say a caption.

Setting the context
Before running this assessment, ensure that the children have been introduced to captions through classroom displays and/or in pictures and books. They should have had opportunities to explore how captions differ from labels and how they give additional information. They should also have had opportunities to count the number of words in captions, and the use of capital letters and full stops, during shared and guided reading sessions. Explain to the children that they are going to look at some pictures with captions. Provide each child with a copy of the photocopiable page 'Captions'. Read through the captions together and discuss the images.

Assessment opportunity
Ask the children to put a circle around the capital letter and full stop in each caption. When they have identified the punctuation in the three captions, invite them to think of a caption for the final picture, count the words and say it to you. After the children have completed the activity, invite them to point out any captions they can see around the classroom. Read these captions together. Ask them to say why they think that captions have been used and not just a label. Make notes of their oral responses against the class list.

Assessment evidence
At level 1, the children will require support in thinking of a caption for the final picture and counting the number of words. At levels 2–3, the children should be able to identify all the capital letters and full stops quickly and make good attempts at saying their own caption for the final picture. Make notes of the children's individual oral responses and use the completed photocopiable page to provide evidence against Reading AF4.

Next steps
Support: In guided reading sessions, encourage the children to identify captions, capital letters and full stops and to think of captions for uncaptioned pictures.
Extension: Encourage the children to write a caption for the final picture on the photocopiable page and use a capital letter and a full stop.

Key aspects of learning
Reasoning: Children will explain why certain labels and captions are appropriate.
Communication: Children will develop their ability to discuss as they work collaboratively in pairs and in a whole-class context. They will communicate outcomes orally, in writing and through ICT if appropriate.

Phase ③ Writing a caption

Learning outcome
Children write a caption for an object or picture in a complete sentence with a capital letter and full stop.

Success criteria
● I can choose a caption for a picture.
● I can write a caption.

Setting the context
The children should have already had experience of writing captions that make sense, using capital letters and full stops, in shared and guided reading. They should understand that a line of writing is not necessarily a sentence and that a sentence can extend over more than one line. They should also have had opportunities to formulate and rehearse making up their own captions with a partner. Display the photocopiable page 'Writing captions' on a whiteboard and read the captions together. Discuss which are appropriate and which are not. Cross out the ones that should be discarded. Invite the children to suggest alternative captions of their own and write them on the board. Ask them to tell you how to punctuate them.

Assessment opportunity
Provide pairs of children with a copy of the photocopiable page 'Caption choices' (version 1 for those at level 1; version 2 for those at levels 2–3). Explain that there are more captions than there are pictures. Ask them to cut out the captions and choose the best one for each picture. Let them stick their chosen captions onto the pictures. They will be left with some to discard. After the children have completed the cut-and-stick activity, ask them to explain why they chose their captions and discarded the others. Observe the children's contributions to the whole-class activity and make notes against the class list.

Assessment evidence
At level 1, the children should be able to give a simple reason for their choices, such as 'It tells a bit more about the picture'. They should also have some awareness of where to use a capital letter and full stop in a sentence. At levels 2–3, the children can explain which of the captions gave relevant information and which were not appropriate. They should also be able to demarcate a sentence correctly with a capital letter and full stop. Use the children's oral responses and cut-and-stick activity to provide evidence against Writing AF2 and AF6.

Next steps
Support: In guided reading, encourage the children to read captions and say what information they add to the picture.
Extension: Invite the children to write captions of their own for the illustrations.

Key aspects of learning
Reasoning: Children will explain why certain labels and captions are appropriate.
Communication: Children will develop their ability to discuss as they work collaboratively in pairs and in a whole-class context. They will communicate outcomes orally, in writing and through ICT if appropriate.

Periodic assessment

Reading

Learning outcome
Children can say what the purposes of lists and labels in the classroom are.

Success criteria
- I know what a label is.
- I know what a list is.
- I know what a caption is.

Setting the context
Ensure that there are a variety of labels, lists and captions visible in different areas of the classroom. Play a 'touch it' game with the children, one group at a time. Call out *label* and challenge a group to find one in as short a time as possible. The children should each, individually, find and touch a label. Once everyone in the group has found a label, ask each child to tell you what the label is for and to read it out, if appropriate. Repeat the game with *list* and then *caption.* Make notes against the class list of the children's oral responses.

Assessment opportunity
This assessment activity gives you the opportunity to check that the children understand the purposes of lists, labels and captions and their differences. You can also take the opportunity to assess the children's ability to listen and respond to an instruction and to read the labels and captions, if appropriate.

Assessment evidence
Make notes of individual responses against the class list and evidence collected during the course of the unit to make evidence against Reading AF4.

Writing

Learning outcome
Children write a caption for an object or picture in a complete sentence with a capital letter and full stop.

Success criteria
I can write labels and captions.

Setting the context
In pairs, ask the children to draw a picture of each other and write a label and a caption for their picture. Collect the children's drawings for a class display. As a plenary session, invite individual children to read the label and caption on their picture and why they chose to write them. Talk to them about what they found difficult about the work in the unit and what they found easy to accomplish. Make notes of their responses against the class list.

Assessment opportunity
This assessment activity provides an opportunity to evaluate the children's understanding of the difference between a label and a caption. It also highlights their understanding of the need for capital letters and full stops when writing a caption, and their own self-awareness of their learning.

Assessment evidence
At level 1, the children may write simple captions. For example, 'This is John'. At levels 2–3, the children will begin to show awareness that captions should provide the reader with additional information. For example, 'This is my best friend'. Make comparisons between your own assessment of the children's writing during this unit and the oral responses of their own achievements. This can be used to provide evidence against Writing AF2 and AF6.

NON-FICTION

Name _____ Date _____

Captions

- Circle the capital letters and full stops.
- Think of a caption for the final picture.

This bedroom has lots of toys.

The farmer looks after the animals.

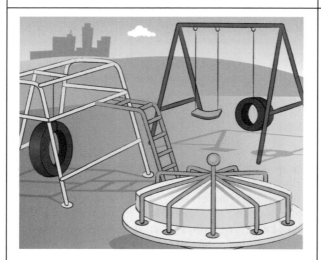

Children can play in playgrounds.

_____
_____

Red
Amber
Green

I can spot capital letters and full stops. ☐
I can think of and say a caption. ☐

PHOTOCOPIABLE ■SCHOLASTIC

Writing captions

Most cars have gears.

This bike has wheels.

Children can play here.

You can see baby animals.

This boy has a new bike.

Bikes like this can be ridden off the road.

Photograph © Carlos Alvarez/www.istockphoto.com.

NON-FICTION
UNIT 2 Instructions (persuasion)

Literacy objectives

Speak and listen for a wide range of purposes in different contexts

Strand 1 Speaking
- Tell stories and describe incidents from their own experience in an audible voice.

Strand 2 Listening and responding
- Listen with sustained concentration, building new stores of words in different contexts.
- Listen to and follow instructions accurately, asking for help and clarification if necessary.

Strand 3 Group discussion and interaction
- Take turns to speak, listen to each other's suggestions and talk about what they are going to do.
- Ask and answer questions, make relevant contributions, offer suggestions and take turns.

Read and write for a range of purposes on paper and on screen

Strand 5 Word recognition: decoding (reading) and encoding (spelling)
- Recognise and use alternative ways of pronouncing the graphemes already taught.
- Recognise and use alternative ways of spelling the phonemes already taught.
- Identify the constituent parts of two-syllable and three-syllable words to support the application of phonic knowledge and skills.
- Recognise automatically an increasing number of familiar high frequency words.
- Apply phonic knowledge and skills as the prime approach to reading and spelling unfamiliar words that are not completely decodable.
- Read more challenging texts which can be decoded using their acquired phonic knowledge and skills, along with automatic recognition of high frequency words.
- Read and spell phonically decodable two-syllable and three-syllable words.

Strand 6 Word structure and spelling
- Spell new words using phonics as the prime approach.
- Segment sounds into their constituent phonemes in order to spell them correctly.
- Recognise and use alternative ways of spelling the graphemes already taught.
- Use knowledge of common inflections in spelling such as plurals, -ly, -er.
- Read and spell phonically decodable two-syllable and three-syllable words.

Strand 7 Understanding and interpreting texts
- Identify the main events and characters in stories, and find specific information in simple texts.
- Recognise the main elements that shape different texts.

Strand 8 Engaging with and responding to texts
- Distinguish fiction and non-fiction texts and the different purposes for reading them.

Strand 9 Creating and shaping texts
- Independently choose what to write about, plan and follow it through.
- Convey information and ideas in simple non-narrative forms.
- Create short simple texts on paper and screen that combine words with images (and sounds).

Strand 10 Text structure and organisation
- Write chronological and non-chronological texts using simple structures.
- Group written sentences together in chunks of meaning or subject.

Strand 11 Sentence structure and punctuation
- Compose and write simple sentences independently to communicate meaning.
- Use capital letters and full stops when punctuating simple sentences.

Strand 12 Presentation
- Use the space bar and keyboard to type their name and simple texts.

Key aspects of learning

Enquiry
● Children will ask questions arising from work on classroom routines and plan how to present this information effectively.

Reasoning
● Children will make judgements on what is fact and what is fiction based on available evidence.

Evaluation
● Children will discuss success criteria for their written work, give feedback to others and judge the effectiveness of their own instructions.

Social skills
● When developing collaborative writing, children will learn about listening to and respecting other people's ideas.

Communication
● Children will develop their ability to discuss as they work collaboratively in paired, group and whole-class contexts. They will communicate outcomes orally, in writing and through ICT if appropriate.

Assessment focuses

Reading
AF4 *(identify and comment on the structure and organisation of texts, including grammatical and presentational features at text level).*
AF5 *(explain and comment on writers' use of language, including grammatical and literary features at word and sentence level).*

Writing
AF2 *(produce texts which are appropriate to task, reader and purpose).*
AF6 *(write with technical accuracy of syntax and punctuation in phrases, clauses and sentences).*

Speaking and listening
Speaking (speak with clarity, intonation and pace).
Listening and responding (listen to others in class, ask relevant questions and follow instructions).
Group discussion and interaction (ask and answer questions, make contributions to sustain an activity, offer suggestions and take turns).

Resources

Phase 1 activities
Interactive activity, 'Labels'
Photocopiable page, 'Labelling a diagram'
Phase 2 activities
Interactive activity, 'Story or instruction?'
Phase 3 activities
Interactive activity, 'Writing instructions'
Photocopiable page, 'Instructions' (versions 1 and 2)

Unit 2 ▢ Instructions (persuasion)

Learning outcomes	Assessment opportunity and evidence	Assessment focuses (AFs)	Success criteria
		Level 1	
Phase ① activity page 88			
Labelling a diagram Children can name the parts of the printer and write simple labels independently.	• Paired activity where children label a printer from a choice of labels on the interactive activity or the photocopiable page. • Paired discussion. • Children's completed interactive activity or photocopiable page and oral responses.	**Writing AF2** Some indication of basic purpose, particular form or awareness of reader.	• I can write simple labels. • I can name the parts of the printer.
Phase ② activities pages 88-89			
Fiction and non-fiction Children can say whether a text is a fiction or a non-fiction text.	• Paired activity where children complete the interactive activity by choosing whether a sentence is fiction or non-fiction. • Paired discussion of the interactive activity. • Children's completed interactive activity and oral responses.	**Reading AF4** Some awareness of meaning of simple text features. **Reading AF5** Comments on obvious features of language.	I can understand the difference between fiction and non-fiction.
Phase ③ activity page 89			
Writing instructions Children can write the next in a sequence of instructions with the support of a partner.	• Paired activity where children choose sentences to fill in gaps on the interactive activity, and then write their own instructions for brushing teeth. • Paired discussion of the interactive activity and role play testing of instructions. • Children's completed interactive activity, photocopiable page and oral responses.	**Writing AF2** Some indication of basic purpose, particular form or awareness of reader. **Writing AF6** • Mostly grammatically accurate clauses. • Some awareness of use of full stops and capital letters.	I can write instructions.

Unit 2 ▢ Instructions (persuasion)

Learning outcomes	Assessment opportunity and evidence	Assessment focuses (AFs)		Success criteria
		Level 2	Level 3	
Phase ① activity page 88				
Labelling a diagram Children can name the parts of the printer and write simple labels independently.	● Independent activity where children label a printer from a choice of labels on the interactive activity or the photocopiable page. ● Children's completed interactive activity or photocopiable page and oral responses.	**Writing AF2** ● Some basic purpose established. ● Some appropriate features of the given form used. ● Some attempts to adopt appropriate style.	**Writing AF2** ● Purpose established at a general level. ● Main features of selected form sometimes signalled to the reader. ● Some attempts at appropriate style, with attention to reader.	● I can write simple labels. ● I can name the parts of the printer.
Phase ② activities pages 88–89				
Fiction and non-fiction Children can say whether a text is a fiction or a non-fiction text.	● Paired activity where children complete the interactive activity by choosing whether a sentence is fiction or non-fiction. ● Paired discussion of the interactive activity. ● Children's completed interactive activity and oral responses.	**Reading AF4** Some awareness of use of features of organisation. **Reading AF5** ● Some effective language choices noted. ● Some familiar patterns of language identified.	**Reading AF4** A few basic features of organisation at text level identified, with little or no linked comment. **Reading AF5** A few basic features of writer's use of language identified, but with little or no comment.	I can understand the difference between fiction and non-fiction.
Phase ③ activity page 89				
Writing instructions Children can add to and write a sequence of instructions.	● Paired activity where children choose sentences to fill in gaps on the interactive activity, and then write their own instructions for brushing teeth. ● Paired discussion of the interactive activity and role play testing of instructions. ● Children's completed interactive activity, photocopiable page and oral responses.	**Writing AF2** ● Some basic purpose established. ● Some appropriate features of the given form used. ● Some attempts to adopt appropriate style. **Writing AF6** ● Clause structure mostly grammatically correct. ● Sentence demarcation with capital letters and full stops usually accurate. ● Some accurate use of question and exclamation marks, and commas in lists.	**Writing AF2** ● Purpose established at a general level. ● Main features of selected form sometimes signalled to the reader. ● Some attempts at appropriate style, with attention to reader. **Writing AF6** ● Straightforward sentences usually demarcated accurately with full stops, capital letters, question and exclamation marks. ● Some, limited, use of speech punctuation. ● Comma splicing evident, particularly in narrative.	I can write instructions.

NON-FICTION

Phase ① Labelling a diagram

Learning outcome
Children can name the parts of the printer and write simple labels independently.

Success criteria
- I can write simple labels.
- I can name the parts of the printer.

Setting the context
Prior to this assessment, the children should have been shown how to operate a computer printer. They will have created their own labels to help them remember simple parts of the printer and used the printer themselves, while naming the parts. Explain to the children that they are going to label a diagram of a printer, using the interactive activity 'Labels' or the photocopiable page 'Labelling a diagram'. Read the list of labels together, before inviting the children to complete the activity.

Assessment opportunity
The children working at level 1 can complete the activity in pairs. At levels 2–3, the children can work independently. When they have labelled their diagrams, ask the children to talk about what they found easy or difficult about the task. Make notes of their oral responses against the class list.

Assessment evidence
At level 1, the children may confuse the labels 'paper tray' and 'paper exit'. At levels 2–3, the children should be able to order and write all the labels correctly. Make notes of the children's oral responses and use these, together with the completed interactive activity, to provide evidence against Writing AF2.

Next steps
Support: Take opportunities to point out labels in other areas of the school and playground. Read them with the children and encourage them to say why labels have been used.
Extension: Encourage the children to write their own labels for diagrams in other areas of the curriculum.

Key aspects of learning
Enquiry: Children will ask questions arising from work on classroom routines and plan how to present this information effectively.
Communication: Children will develop their ability to discuss as they work collaboratively in paired, group and whole-class contexts. They will communicate outcomes orally, in writing and through ICT if appropriate.

Phase ② Fiction and non-fiction

Learning outcome
Children can say whether a text is a fiction or a non-fiction text.

Success criteria
I can understand the difference between fiction and non-fiction.

Setting the context
The children should have completed the previous activity. They should also have had plenty of opportunities to compare instruction texts with stories and poems, and become familiar with the sentence constructions that are typical of instructions. In pairs, invite the children to complete the interactive activity 'Story or instruction?'.

Assessment opportunity
Assess the children's ability to differentiate between fiction and non-fiction. Discuss the interactive activity with the children. Ask them to explain how they decided if a sentence was from a non-fiction or a fiction text. Make notes of their responses.

Assessment evidence
At level 1, the children may confuse examples in the activity that both use 'You' to begin the sentence. At levels 2-3, the children should be able to differentiate between most of the pairs of sentences. Use the completed interactive activity and the children's oral responses to provide evidence against Reading AF4 and AF5.

Next steps
Support: In guided reading sessions, encourage the children to talk about the order of the words in an instruction text to help them recognise instructions.
Extension: Discuss examples of instructions that use different styles. For example, one word commands, such as 'Start', and persuasive instructions, such as 'Don't miss this amazing offer'.

Key aspects of learning
Reasoning: Children will make judgements on what is fact and what is fiction based on available evidence.

Phase ③ Writing instructions

Learning outcome
Children can write the next in a sequence of instructions, with the support of a partner.

Success criteria
I can write instructions.

Setting the context
Prior to this assessment, the children should have had the opportunity to write instructions, and have been given practice in the use of instructional language. In pairs, provide the children with the interactive activity 'Writing instructions'. Invite them to complete the activity by choosing the next two steps in the sequence.

Assessment opportunity
Ask the pairs to describe how they chose the correct instructions. Then, provide the children with individual copies of the photocopiable page 'Instructions'. Ask them to write instructions for each of the three pictures. The children working at level 1 are provided with some useful words to help them (on version 1). At levels 2-3, the children should attempt to write a sentence for each image (on version 2). After the children have completed their instructions, invite them to swap their pages with a partner and role play following each other's instructions to see if they are effective.

Assessment evidence
At level 1, the children should be able to write one instruction with the support of a wordbank. At levels 2-3, the children can write two or more instructions using words from their own knowledge and experience. Use the children's paired responses, completed interactive activity and photocopiable pages as evidence against Writing AF2 and AF6.

Next steps
Support: Give the children regular practice at following a set of instructions. Draw their attention to sentence construction and the way instructions are sequenced.
Extension: Encourage the children to write a more detailed set of instructions for cleaning teeth, providing more than three steps.

Key aspects of learning
Evaluation: Children will discuss success criteria for their written work, give feedback to others and judge the effectiveness of their own instructions.
Social skills: When developing collaborative writing, children will learn about listening to and respecting other people's ideas.

NON-FICTION

Periodic assessment

Reading

Learning outcomes
● Children can say whether a text is a fiction or non-fiction text.
● Children can listen to and follow simple instructions.

Success criteria
● I can understand the difference between fiction and non-fiction.
● I can follow simple instructions.

Setting the context
Provide groups of children with several books from the class or school library. Invite them to look at the text and illustrations in each book and group them into two piles: fiction and non-fiction. When each group has finished, ask them to give reasons for their choices. Make notes of their responses. Next, put the children into pairs and invite them to play a short barrier game. Ask one child in each pair to draw a simple picture and, as they draw, give instructions to their partner who must try and produce a similar picture. Ask them to compare both drawings afterwards to check that the instructions have been followed correctly. Invite the children to feed back their responses to the activity by asking: *Were the instructions clear? Were they easy or hard to follow? Was anything missed out?*

Assessment opportunity
The first assessment activity gives you the opportunity to assess whether the children understand the difference between fiction and non-fiction texts. The barrier game gives you the opportunity to assess the children's ability to give clear instructions, and to listen to and respond to an instruction.

Assessment evidence
Make notes of the groups' responses against the class list. Use this together with evidence collected during the course of the unit to provide evidence against Reading AF4.

Writing

Learning outcome
Children can write at least three instructions in a well-rehearsed sequence independently.

Success criteria
I can write instructions.

Setting the context
Collect the writing that was done during the course of the unit and review these pieces with the individual children. Invite them to tell you what they know about writing instructions that they did not know at the start of the unit. Make notes of their responses against the class list.

Assessment opportunity
Invite the children to use the completed photocopiable page 'Labelling a diagram' (from the phase 1 activity), and add at least two instructions for operating a printer. Ask them to swap their instructions with a partner to see if the partner can follow them. Invite them to express their opinions about the need for a labelled diagram to accompany instructions. Ask: *Does it make the instructions easier to follow?*

Assessment evidence
At level 1, the children may write two instructions. At levels 2–3, the children will write three or more instructions and will know the importance of clarity and sequence. Use this to provide evidence against Writing AF2, AF6 and AF7.

Name	Date

Labelling a diagram

◤ Label the printer.

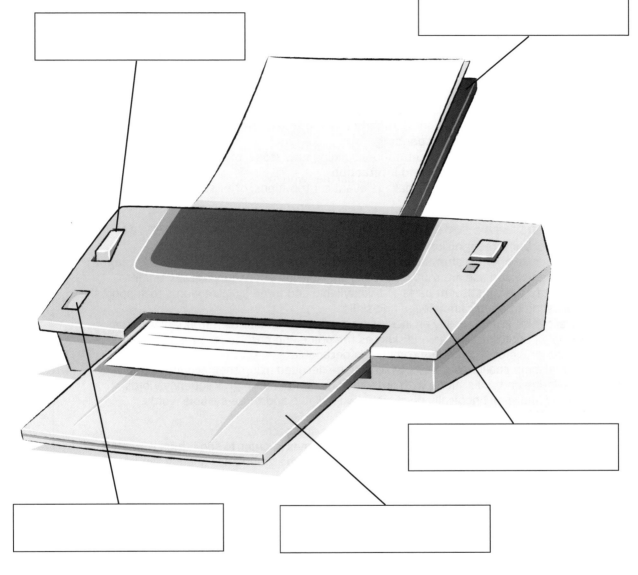

printer	paper tray	light

on button	paper exit

Red
Amber
Green

I can name the parts of the printer. ☐

NON-FICTION

NON-FICTION
UNIT 3 Recount, dictionary

Literacy objectives

Speak and listen for a wide range of purposes in different contexts
Strand 1 Speaking
- Tell stories and describe incidents from their own experience in an audible voice.

Strand 2 Listening and responding
- Listen with sustained concentration, building new stores of words in different contexts.

Strand 3 Group discussion and interaction
- Ask and answer questions, make relevant contributions, offer suggestions and take turns.

Read and write for a range of purposes on paper and on screen
Strand 5 Word recognition: decoding (reading) and encoding (spelling)
- Recognise and use alternative ways of pronouncing the graphemes already taught.
- Recognise and use alternative ways of spelling the phonemes already taught.
- Identify the constituent parts of two-syllable and three-syllable words to support the application of phonic knowledge and skills.
- Recognise automatically an increasing number of familiar high frequency words.
- Apply phonic knowledge and skills as the prime approach to reading and spelling unfamiliar words that are not completely decodable.
- Read more challenging texts which can be decoded using their acquired phonic knowledge and skills, along with automatic recognition of high frequency words.
- Read and spell phonically decodable two-syllable and three-syllable words.

Strand 6 Word structure and spelling
- Spell new words using phonics as the prime approach.
- Segment sounds into their constituent phonemes in order to spell them correctly.
- Recognise and use alternative ways of spelling the graphemes already taught.
- Use knowledge of common inflections in spelling, such as plurals, -ly, -er.
- Read and spell phonically decodable two-syllable and three-syllable words.

Strand 7 Understanding and interpreting texts
- Identify the main events and characters in stories, and find specific information in simple texts.
- Recognise the main elements that shape different texts.

Strand 8 Engaging with and responding to texts
- Visualise and comment on events, characters and ideas, making imaginative links to their own experiences.

Strand 9 Creating and shaping texts
- Independently choose what to write about, plan and follow it through.
- Convey information and ideas in simple non-narrative forms.
- Create short simple texts on paper and screen that combine words with images (and sounds).

Strand 10 Text structure and organisation
- Write chronological and non-chronological texts using simple structures.
- Group written sentences together in chunks of meaning or subject.

Strand 11 Sentence structure and punctuation
- Compose and write simple sentences independently to communicate meaning.
- Use capital letters and full stops when punctuating simple sentences.

Strand 12 Presentation
- Use the space bar and keyboard to type their name and simple texts.

Key aspects of learning

Enquiry
- Children will ask questions arising from visits and/or events and activities in order to add greater detail.

Reasoning
- Children will decide how to order recounts. They will learn to structure their speaking and writing into chronological order.

Evaluation
- Children will discuss success criteria for their written work, give feedback to others and begin to judge the effectiveness of their own recounts.

Social skills
- When developing collaborative writing, children will learn about listening to and respecting other people's ideas.

Communication
- Children will develop their ability to discuss as they work collaboratively in paired, group and whole-class contexts. They will communicate outcomes orally, in writing and through ICT if appropriate.

Assessment focuses

Reading

AF2 *(understand, describe, select or retrieve information, events or ideas from texts and use quotation and reference to text).*

AF4 *(identify and comment on the structure and organisation of texts, including grammatical and presentational features at text level).*

Writing

AF3 *(organise and present whole texts effectively, sequencing and structuring information, ideas and events).*

AF6 *(write with technical accuracy of syntax and punctuation in phrases, clauses and sentences).*

Speaking and listening

Speaking (speak with clarity, intonation and pace).

Listening and responding (listen with sustained concentration).

Group discussion and interaction (ask and answer questions, make relevant contributions to sustain an activity, offer suggestions and take turns).

Resources

Phase 1 activities
Photocopiable page, 'The shopping trip '
Interactive activity, 'Questions and answers'

Phase 2 activities
Interactive activity, 'Sequencing a recount'
Photocopiable page, 'Sequencing a recount'

Phase 3 activities
Interactive activity, 'Making a dictionary'
Photocopiable page, 'Recount frame'

Periodic assessment
Photocopiable page, 'Non-fiction 3 Reading assessment'

Unit 3 🔲 Recount, dictionary

Learning outcomes	Assessment opportunity and evidence	Assessment focuses (AFs)	Success criteria
		Level 1	
Phase ① activity page 96			
Questions and answers Children can listen to a recount and ask questions to support their understanding.	● Group activity where children respond to a pictorial recount, asking questions and giving answers. ● Group discussion and oral responses to the pictorial recount.	**Reading AF2** ● Some simple points from familiar texts recalled. ● Some pages/sections of interest located.	I can ask questions about a recount.
Phase ② activity page 97			
Sequencing ● Children can order events correctly. ● Children can identify and explain the main features of a sentence.	● Paired activity where children sequence sentences for a recount and identify time connectives. ● Paired discussion of the sequencing activity. ● Children's completed photocopiable page/interactive activity and oral responses.	**Reading AF4** Some awareness of meaning of simple text features. **Writing AF3** ● Some formulaic phrases indicate start/end of text. ● Events/ideas sometimes in appropriate order.	I can put sentences in the correct order to tell a recount.
Phase ③ activity page 98			
Writing recounts ● Children can use knowledge of the alphabet to locate words in simple dictionaries. ● Children can write at least three simple sentences in the past tense and use some time connectives in a recount.	● Independent activity where children do an interactive activity to demonstrate how words in a dictionary are ordered. They then draw and write notes for a recount. ● Individual oral presentation of a recount. ● Children's completed interactive activity, notes and drawings on the photocopiable page and oral responses.	**Writing AF6** ● Mostly grammatically accurate clauses. ● Some awareness of use of full stops and capital letters.	● I can use a dictionary. ● I can plan a recount. ● I can write sentences using full stops and capital letters.

Unit 3 ⬜ Recount, dictionary

Learning outcomes	Assessment opportunity and evidence	Assessment focuses (AFs)		Success criteria
		Level 2	**Level 3**	
Phase ① activity page 96				
Questions and answers Children can listen to a recount and ask questions to support their understanding.	• Group activity where children respond to a pictorial recount, asking questions and giving answers. • Group discussion and oral responses to the pictorial recount.	**Reading AF2** • Some specific, straightforward information recalled. • Generally clear idea of where to look for information.	**Reading AF2** • Simple, most obvious points identified though there may also be some misunderstanding. • Some comments include quotations from or references to text, but not always relevant.	I can ask questions about a recount.
Phase ② activity page 97				
Sequencing • Children can order events correctly. • Children can identify and explain the main features of a sentence.	• Independent activity where children sequence sentences for a recount and identify time connectives. • Children's completed photocopiable page/interactive activity and oral responses.	**Writing AF3** • Some basic sequencing of ideas or material. • Openings and/or closings sometimes signalled. **Reading AF4** Some awareness of use of features of organisation.	**Writing AF3** • Some attempt to organise ideas with related points placed next to each other. • Openings and closings usually signalled. • Some attempt to sequence ideas or material logically. **Reading AF4** A few basic features of organisation at text level identified, with little or no linked comment.	I can put sentences in the correct order to tell a recount.
Phase ③ activity page 98				
Writing recounts • Children can use knowledge of the alphabet to locate words in simple dictionaries. • Children can write at least three simple sentences in the past tense and use some time connectives in a recount.	• Independent activity where children do an interactive activity to demonstrate how words in a dictionary are ordered. They then draw and write notes and sentences for a recount. • Individual oral presentation of a recount. • Children's completed interactive activity, notes and drawings on the photocopiable page and oral responses.	**Writing AF6** • Clause structure mostly grammatically correct. • Sentence demarcation with capital letters and full stops usually accurate. • Some accurate use of question and exclamation marks, and commas in lists.	**Writing AF6** • Straightforward sentences usually demarcated accurately with full stops, capital letters, question and exclamation marks. • Some, limited, use of speech punctuation. • Comma splicing evident, particularly in narrative.	• I can use a dictionary. • I can plan a recount. • I can write sentences using full stops and capital letters.

Phase ① Questions and answers

Learning outcome
Children can listen to a recount and ask questions to support their understanding.

Success criteria
I can ask questions about a recount.

Setting the context
This assessment should be carried out after the children have listened to a recount in the past tense and have had an opportunity to ask and answer questions about it with a partner.

Assessment opportunity
Invite the children to work in small, mixed-ability groups using the photocopiable page 'The shopping trip'. Explain that the pictures provide a recount of what happened when a family went shopping last weekend. Be sure to emphasise the past tense. Group members should take turns to ask and answer questions about what happened in each picture using past-tense verbs.

Assessment evidence
When working in groups, the children at levels 2–3 will use the past tense for their questions and answers, while the children at level 1 may occasionally need prompting. Make notes of the children's responses and use these to provide evidence against Reading AF2.

Next steps
Support: Take opportunities to talk to the children about things they have done in the past to encourage them to use past-tense verbs. Ask them questions about the events to help them recount in a logical sequence.
Extension: Invite the children to do the interactive activity 'Questions and answers'. To complete the activity they will need to add the correct punctuation to a series of sentences.

Key aspects of learning
Enquiry: Children will ask questions arising from visits and/or events and activities in order to add greater detail.
Evaluation: Children will discuss success criteria for their written work, give feedback to others and begin to judge the effectiveness of their own recounts.
Social skills: When developing collaborative writing, children will learn about listening to and respecting other people's ideas.
Communication: Children will develop their ability to discuss as they work collaboratively in paired, group and whole-class contexts. They will communicate outcomes orally, in writing and through ICT if appropriate.

NON-FICTION

Phase ② Sequencing

Learning outcomes
- Children can order events correctly.
- Children can identify and explain the main features of a sentence.

Success criteria
I can put sentences in the correct order to tell a recount.

Setting the context
This assessment activity should be undertaken once the children have had opportunities to draw a sequence of pictures about a recount, or drawn a timeline to sequence a recount. They should have had the opportunity to write at least two sentences to accompany the pictures. They should also have revised the construction of sentences and had the opportunity to explore time connectives during supported composition.

Assessment opportunity
Provide the children with a copy of the photocopiable page 'Sequencing a recount' or the interactive version. Ask them to put the six sentences in the correct order. The children at level 1 can complete the activity with a partner. Afterwards, ask the children to read their choices aloud to check that their sentences are in the correct order. Hold a plenary and discuss the activity with the children. Ask them to explain how they decided on the order of the sentences. Ask them to read the words that indicated the correct order. Make notes of their oral responses against the class list.

Assessment evidence
At level 1, the children will be able to sequence most of their recount by finding time connectives at the beginning of sentences. At levels 2-3, the children will focus more on the content of the sentences to order the recount. Make notes of the children's individual oral responses and use the completed interactive activity or photocopiable page to provide evidence against Reading AF4 and Writing AF3.

Next steps
Support: Encourage the children to find time connectives during guided reading sessions and in other areas of the curriculum.
Extension: Encourage the children to collect time connectives and write them in personal wordbanks for use in writing.

Key aspects of learning
Reasoning: Children will decide how to order recounts. They will learn to structure their speaking and writing into chronological order.
Social skills: When developing collaborative writing, children will learn about listening to and respecting other people's ideas.
Communication: Children will develop their ability to discuss as they work collaboratively in paired, group and whole-class contexts. They will communicate outcomes orally, in writing and through ICT if appropriate.

Phase ③ Writing recounts

Learning outcomes
● Children can use knowledge of the alphabet to locate words in simple dictionaries.
● Children can write at least three simple sentences in the past tense and use some time connectives in a recount.

Success criteria
● I can use a dictionary.
● I can plan a recount.
● I can write sentences using full stops and capital letters.

Setting the context
Prior to this assessment, the children should have had experience of using dictionaries. They should also have identified and recorded the main features of a recount text and made lists of useful time-related words. They will also have generated a list of success criteria for a recount text from their shared reading.

Assessment opportunity
Invite the children to complete the interactive activity 'Making a dictionary'. This will assess the children's understanding of a dictionary format and their ability to place words in alphabetical order. Afterwards, provide them with the photocopiable page 'Recount frame'. Read the headings on the page and explain to the children that they are to draw and write notes for a recount about one of the topics discussed during the course of the unit, using the frame for planning. When the children have had sufficient time to draw and write their ideas, ask them to use the notes to orally describe their recount. Encourage them to use time-related words to sequence their retelling. Afterwards, hold a plenary and encourage the children to say if and how using a frame made it easier to order and present their recounts.

Assessment evidence
At level 1, the children should be able to write one sentence with a capital letter and full stop. At levels 2–3, the children should write three sentences, correctly punctuated. The completed photocopiable pages and children's oral retellings can be used to provide evidence against Writing AF6.

Next steps
Support: Use an enlarged version of the recount frame and work with the children to draw and/or write a piece of information under each heading. Model how to write a sentence based on the notes that you have made.
Extension: Encourage the children to use their notes to write a full version of their recount.

Key aspects of learning
Reasoning: Children will decide how to order recounts. They will learn to structure their speaking and writing into chronological order.
Evaluation: Children will discuss success criteria for their written work, give feedback to others and begin to judge the effectiveness of their own recounts.
Social skills: When developing collaborative writing, children will learn about listening to and respecting other people's ideas.
Communication: Children will develop their ability to discuss as they work collaboratively in paired, group and whole-class contexts. They will communicate outcomes orally, in writing and through ICT if appropriate.

Periodic assessment

Reading

Learning outcome
Children can use knowledge of the alphabet to locate words in simple dictionaries.

Success criteria
I can use a dictionary.

Setting the context
Perform this assessment with small groups of children. Provide each child with a dictionary. Prepare a set of word cards, featuring words that will be useful for the children when writing recounts in the future. A range is available on the photocopiable page 'Non-fiction 3 Reading assessment'.

Assessment opportunity
Hold up the cards one at a time and ask the children to read them aloud. Ask them to say if they have used the word in any of their recount writing during this unit and to say a sentence using the word. When they have read all the words, hold them up again in a different order and challenge the children to find each word in a dictionary. Repeat the activity, putting the words in a new order, and encourage the children to see who can be the first to find and read each word in their dictionary.

Assessment evidence
Observe and make notes of individual children's responses against the class list. Use this together with evidence collected during the course of the unit to provide evidence against Reading AF1.

Writing

Learning outcome
Children can write at least three simple sentences in the past tense and use some time connectives in a recount.

Success criteria
I can write sentences using full stops and capital letters.

Setting the context
Collect the writing that was done during the course of the unit and review these pieces with the children, individually. Talk to them about what they found difficult about the work and what they found easy.

Assessment opportunity
Ask the children to use their notes and pictures for planning a recount from earlier in the unit, and then write three new sentences about the event. Ask them to swap with a partner and compare the new sentences with the original ones that they wrote. Invite the partner to say if they have improved their sentence writing and how. For example, 'Have they remembered to use capital letters and full stops? Have they used time connectives?' Invite them to tell you what they know about writing recounts that they did not know at the start of the unit and make notes of their responses.

Assessment evidence
At level 1, the children may forget to use capital letters and full stops when writing their sentences. At level 2, the children will use capital letters and full stops more consistently, while those at level 3 will use more sophisticated punctuation, including commas and exclamation marks. Make comparisons between your own evidence gathered during this unit with the children's oral assessment of their own achievements and the peer evaluations. This can be used to provide evidence against Writing AF6.

NON-FICTION

Name	Date

The shopping trip

◼ Take turns to ask and answer questions about what happened in these pictures.

I can ask questions about a recount. ◻

Red
Amber
Green

Illustrations © 2010, Anna Godwin/The Illustrator Agency.

Non-fiction 3 Reading assessment

first	next	after
when	later	last
said	then	went
saw	played	told

NON-FICTION

UNIT 4 Information texts (dictionaries, fact and fiction, report)

Literacy objectives

Speak and listen for a wide range of purposes in different contexts

Strand 2 Listening and responding
- Listen with sustained concentration, building new stores of words in different contexts.
- Listen to tapes or video and express views about how a story or information has been presented.

Strand 3 Group discussion and interaction
- Ask and answer questions, make relevant contributions, offer suggestions and take turns.

Read and write for a range of purposes on paper and on screen

Strand 6 Word structure and spelling
- Spell new words using phonics as the prime approach.
- Segment sounds into their constituent phonemes in order to spell them correctly.
- Recognise and use alternative ways of spelling the graphemes already taught.
- Use knowledge of common inflections in spelling, such as plurals, -*ly*, -*er*.
- Read and spell phonically decodable two-syllable and three-syllable words.

Strand 7 Understanding and interpreting texts
- Make predictions showing an understanding of ideas, events and characters.
- Recognise the main elements that shape different texts.

Strand 8 Engaging with and responding to texts
- Select books for personal reading and give reasons for choices.

Strand 9 Creating and shaping texts
- Independently choose what to write about, plan and follow it through.
- Convey information and ideas in simple non-narrative forms.
- Find and use new and interesting words and phrases, including story language.
- Create short simple texts on paper and screen that combine words with images (and sounds).

Strand 10 Text structure and organisation
- Write chronological and non-chronological texts using simple structures.
- Group written sentences together in chunks of meaning or subject.

Strand 11 Sentence structure and punctuation
- Compose and write simple sentences independently to communicate meaning.
- Use capital letters and full stops when punctuating simple sentences.

Key aspects of learning

Enquiry
- Children will ask questions arising from work in another area of the curriculum, for example on wheeled toys. They will ask relevant questions about why things happen and how they work, and explore how to find the answers using different sources of information.

Information processing
- Children will use first-hand experience and simple information sources to answer questions. They will learn where to find information and understand what is relevant..

Reasoning
- Children will develop their concepts of fact and fiction and be able to explain why they have categorised a particular text.

Evaluation
- Children will present information orally and in writing. They will discuss success criteria and judge the effectiveness of their own work.

Social skills
- When developing collaborative writing, children will learn about listening to and respecting other people's ideas.

Communication
- Children will develop their ability to discuss as they work collaboratively. They will communicate outcomes orally, in writing and through ICT if appropriate.

Assessment focuses

Reading
AF2 *(understand, describe, select or retrieve information, events or ideas from texts and use quotation and reference to text).*
AF4 *(identify and comment on the structure and organisation of texts, including grammatical and presentational features at text level).*

Writing
AF5 *(vary sentences for clarity, purpose and effect).*

Speaking and listening
Listening and responding (listen with sustained concentration and express views on the presentation of information).
Group discussion and interaction (ask and answer questions, make relevant contributions to sustain an activity, offer suggestions and take turns).

Resources

Phase 1 activities
Interactive activity, 'Creating an index'
Photocopiable page, 'Where can I find the answers?' (versions 1 and 2)
Phase 2 activities
Interactive activity, 'Fiction or non-fiction?'
Phase 3 activities
Interactive activity, 'Report or recount?'
Photocopiable page, 'Toys' (versions 1 and 2)
Periodic assessment
Photocopiable page, 'Non-fiction 4 Reading assessment'
Photocopiable page, 'Non-fiction 4 Writing assessment text'

Unit 4 ▭ Information texts (dictionaries, fact and fiction, report)

Learning outcomes	Assessment opportunity and evidence	Assessment focuses (AFs)		Success criteria
		Level 1		

Phase ① activity page 106

Learning outcomes	Assessment opportunity and evidence	Assessment focuses (AFs) Level 1	Success criteria
Finding information • Children can ask simple questions. • Children can identify a contents page and an index in an information text. They can use these to find the right page to answer simple questions.	• Paired activity where children order words to create an index. They then identify which pages in an index they would use to find out information and answer simple questions. • Paired discussion of the interactive activity, and children's questions and oral responses when using the index. • Children's completed interactive activity, photocopiable page and oral responses.	**Reading AF2** • Some simple points from familiar texts recalled. • Some pages/sections of interest located.	• I can ask simple questions. • I can use an index to find information. • I know the order of the alphabet.

Phase ② activity page 107

Fiction or non-fiction? Children can say what the key structural features of a simple information text are.	• Paired activity where children explore a number of words, phrases and titles, and decide which type of text they belong to. • Paired discussion of the interactive task and feedback afterwards. • Children's completed interactive activity and oral responses.	**Reading AF4** Some awareness of meaning of simple text features.	• I know the difference between fact and fiction. • I can identify the features of an information text.

Phase ③ activity page 108

Reports Children can write sentences for an information text in an appropriate style.	• Paired and supported group activity where children categorise verbs for reports and recounts and rewrite sentences for a report text. • Paired and group work discussion, categorising verbs and rewriting sentences. • Children's completed interactive activity, photocopiable page and self-assessment.	**Writing AF5** • Reliance on simple phrases and clauses. • Some sentence-like structures formed by chaining clauses together.	I can write a report text.

Unit 4 📖 Information texts (dictionaries, fact and fiction, report)

Learning outcomes	Assessment opportunity and evidence	Assessment focuses (AFs)		Success criteria
		Level 2	Level 3	
Phase ① activity page 106				
Finding information • Children can ask simple questions. • Children can identify a contents page and an index in an information text. They can use these to find the right page to answer simple questions.	• Paired activity where children order words to create an index. They then identify which pages in an index they would use to find out information and answer simple questions. • Paired discussion of the interactive activity, and children's questions and oral responses when using the index. • Children's completed interactive activity, photocopiable page and oral responses.	**Reading AF2** • Some specific, straightforward information recalled. • Generally clear idea of where to look for information.	**Reading AF2** • Simple, most obvious points identified though there may also be some misunderstanding. • Some comments include quotations from or references to text, but not always relevant.	• I can ask simple questions. • I can use an index to find information. • I know the order of the alphabet.
Phase ② activity page 107				
Fiction or non-fiction Children can say what the key structural features of a simple information text are.	• Paired and/or independent activity where children explore a number of words, phrases and titles, and decide which type of text they belong to. • Paired discussion of the interactive task and feedback afterwards. • Children's completed interactive activity and oral responses.	**Reading AF4** Some awareness of use of features of organisation.	**Reading AF4** A few basic features of organisation at text level identified, with little or no linked comment.	• I know the difference between fact and fiction. • I can identify the features of an information text.
Phase ③ activity page 108				
Reports Children can write sentences for an information text in an appropriate style.	• Independent and paired activity where children categorise verbs for reports and recounts and rewrite sentences for a report text. • Children's completed interactive activity, photocopiable page and self-assessment.	**Writing AF5** • Some variation in sentence openings. • Mainly simple sentences with *and* used to connect clauses. • Past and present tense generally consistent.	**Writing AF5** • Reliance mainly on simply structured sentences, variation with support. • *and, but, so* are the most common connectives, subordination occasionally. • Some limited variation in use of tense and verb forms, not always secure.	I can write a report text.

NON-FICTION

Phase ① Finding information

Learning outcomes
● Children can ask simple questions.
● Children can identify a contents page and an index in an information text. They can use these to find the right page to answer simple questions.

Success criteria
● I can ask simple questions.
● I can use an index to find information.
● I know the order of the alphabet.

Setting the context
This assessment should be carried out once the children have investigated using the features of non-fiction texts to find the answers to simple questions about a topic. They will have explored how to use the contents page and the index of non-fiction books, and will have used a glossary to help them understand the meaning of the answers in the text.

Assessment opportunity
In pairs, invite the children to complete the interactive activity 'Creating an index'. The children must work with their partner to put the jumbled-up index into alphabetical order. Next, invite them to complete the photocopiable page 'Where can I find the answers?' (versions 1 and 2). Using the index on the page, the children must work out which pages they should turn to in the book to find the information they need. Ask the children to explain why some entries in the index have more than one page reference. For those using version 2 of the photocopiable page, invite them to explain how they found the page about bicycle tyres. Make notes of their oral responses against the class list. Afterwards, invite the children to think of two related questions to ask their partner, who must then show which part of the index they would use to find the answers.

Assessment evidence
At level 1, the children may struggle when ordering words using the second letter. For example, 'car' and 'cog'. At levels 2-3, the children will be more confident in ordering the words and will be able to give a simple explanation of where to find pages using an index. Use the children's oral responses, completed interactive activity and photocopiable pages to provide evidence against Reading AF2.

Next steps
Support: In guided reading sessions, invite the children to think of a question and try to find the relevant page using the index.
Extension: Provide opportunities for the children to order words by first, second and third letter of the alphabet.

Key aspects of learning
Enquiry: Children will ask questions arising from work in another area of the curriculum, for example on wheeled toys. They will ask relevant questions about why things happen and how they work, and explore how to find the answers using different sources of information.
Communication: Children will develop their ability to discuss as they work collaboratively in paired, group and whole-class contexts. They will communicate outcomes orally, in writing and through ICT if appropriate.

Phase ② Fiction or non-fiction?

Learning outcome
Children can say what the key structural features of a simple information text are.

Success criteria
- I know the difference between fact and fiction.
- I can identify the features of an information text.

Setting the context
Prior to this assessment, the children should have explored a range of non-fiction texts and completed activities that require the use of an index, contents page and glossary. They should also have compared fiction and non-fiction texts and discussed how the language and punctuation differs.

Assessment opportunity
Invite the children to work with a partner to complete the interactive activity 'Fiction or non-fiction?'. Tell them to read and discuss the titles, sentences and language features, then to agree on which type of text each one is. The children working at level 3 can do the activity independently. Afterwards, ask the children to feed back on the activity. What did they find easy or hard? Encourage them to explain how they arrived at each of their answers. Make notes of their oral responses against the class list.

Assessment evidence
At level 1, the children may suggest that a sentence belongs to a story because it uses words like 'angry'. They may be less confident at working out which titles are fiction and non-fiction. At levels 2–3, the children may suggest that a sentence is non-fiction because it tells you about something that really happened, or is fiction because it has speech marks in it. Use children's oral responses and the completed interactive activity to provide evidence against Reading AF4.

Next steps
Support: If the children have difficulty in differentiating between fiction and non-fiction, let them investigate what is similar about a collection of non-fiction books and then a group of fiction books, before asking them to find the differences.
Extension: Encourage the children to categorise a selection of non-fiction books by their differences.

Key aspects of learning
Reasoning: Children will develop their concepts of fact and fiction and be able to explain why they have categorised a particular text.
Communication: Children will develop their ability to discuss as they work collaboratively in paired, group and whole-class contexts. They will communicate outcomes orally, in writing and through ICT if appropriate.

Phase ③ Reports

Learning outcome
Children can write sentences for an information text in an appropriate style.

Success criteria
I can write a report text.

Setting the context
The children should have previously explored the features of a report text, including layout, headings, introductions and use of present-tense verbs. Remind them of the work that they produced for Non-fiction Unit 3. Look back at examples of recount texts and talk about their purpose and their use of past-tense verbs.

Assessment opportunity
In pairs, invite the children to complete the interactive activity 'Report or recount?'. The children at level 3 can work independently. Then, provide the children with individual copies of the photocopiable page 'Toys' (version 1 or 2). Ask them to read the sentences and then rewrite them in a style more appropriate for a report text. At level 1, the children should work in a supported group using version 1 of the photocopiable page. Once they have completed their sentences, invite the children to read them out to a partner. Ask them to evaluate their own sentences afterwards, as a result of comparing them with their partner's. Make notes of their oral responses against the class list.

Assessment evidence
At level 1, the children should recognise most past-tense and present-tense verbs. When writing their sentences, they may include the past tense and forget to replace adjectives. At levels 2–3, the children will be confident in using the correct tense and write more appropriate sentences. Use the children's completed interactive activity and photocopiable page to provide evidence against Writing AF5.

Next steps
Support: In guided reading sessions, provide the children with further opportunities to study the features and language of report texts.
Extension: Invite the children to rewrite the sentences on the photocopiable page as a paragraph and add two more sentences.

Key aspects of learning
Reasoning: Children will develop their concepts of fact and fiction and be able to explain why they have categorised a particular text.
Evaluation: Children will present information orally and in writing. They will discuss success criteria and judge the effectiveness of their own work.
Social skills: When developing collaborative writing, children will learn about listening to and respecting other people's ideas.
Communication: Children will develop their ability to discuss as they work collaboratively in paired, group and whole-class contexts. They will communicate outcomes orally, in writing and through ICT if appropriate.

Periodic assessment

Reading

Learning outcome
Children can say what the key structural features of a simple information text are.

Success criteria
- I can identify the features of an information text.
- I know the difference between fact and fiction.

Setting the context
Provide the children with a mixed selection of story and information books. Challenge them to find the following features (choosing a different book each time): contents page; glossary; index; label; caption; sentence in the present tense; fictional character; past-tense sentence. As they find an example, ask them to read it aloud and say if it is fiction or non-fiction.

Assessment opportunity
Invite the groups to cut out the labels on the photocopiable page 'Non-fiction 4 Reading assessment' and collect the statements that refer to information texts, discarding those that don't. Ask them to glue their chosen statements onto a sheet of paper to create a checklist of features. Encourage them to explain why certain statements were discarded. Make notes of individual and group responses against the class list.

Assessment evidence
Use the children's oral responses, checklists and evidence collected during the course of the unit to provide evidence against Reading AF4 and AF5.

Writing

Learning outcome
Children can write sentences for an information text in an appropriate style.

Success criteria
I can write report text using appropriate sentences.

Setting the context
Provide the children with a copy of the report text skeleton on the photocopiable page 'Non-fiction 4 Writing assessment' or display a version on the whiteboard.

Assessment opportunity
Invite the children to use the notes on the skeleton to write at least one complete sentence for each point in the circles. The children at levels 1–2 can work in pairs. When they have finished, ask the children to talk about what they found difficult about the work in the unit and what they found easy to accomplish. Make notes of their responses against the class list.

Assessment evidence
At level 1, the children may write simple sentences that fail to give additional information about the points in the circles. For example, 'Toys with wheels are cars'. At levels 2–3, the children will demonstrate an ability to give additional information in their sentences. For example, 'Many toys have wheels. One sort of toy with wheels is a scooter. Scooters are fun'. Make comparisons between your own assessment of children's writing during this unit with their oral self-assessment. This can be used to provide evidence against Writing AF2.

NON-FICTION

Name	Date

Where can I find the answers? (1)

◼ Read the index for the book *All About Wheels*.

Index

bicycles	2, 5, 14
cars	2, 7, 14
cogs	14
early wheels	5
gears	14
scooters	9
trains	11
tyres	5, 7, 9

◼ Write the page numbers to show where you would find out about these:

scooters _____

bicycles _____

cars _____

gears _____

cogs _____

Red
Amber
Green

I can use an index to find information. ☐

NON-FICTION

Name	Date

Toys (1)

We all like playing with toys.

> The football came from a sports shop.
>
> My football was black and white.
>
> Teddy bears are very cute and cuddly.
>
> Dolls can be dressed up in lots of pretty clothes.
>
> Some toy cars are really tiny.

◼ Rewrite the sentences for a report about toys:

Footballs come from a sports shop.

_____

_____

_____

_____

_____

Red
Amber
Green

I can write a report text. ☐

Ball © Photodisc Inc./Getty images; bear © Photo.com /JupiterImages; car © 2006 Christine Glade; doll © Graham Mitchell/www.istockphoto.com.

Non-fiction 4 Reading assessment

◗ Cut out the cards. Read the features and decide if they belong in a report text.

◗ Glue them onto a sheet of paper to make a report checklist.

General nouns	Time connectives (first, next, last)	Third person (he, she, they or it. Not I or we)
Present tense (are, is, have)	Past tense (was, saw, went)	Contents page
Index	Made-up characters	Facts
Headings	Captions	Photo-graphs

Non-fiction 4 Writing assessment text

Report text skeleton

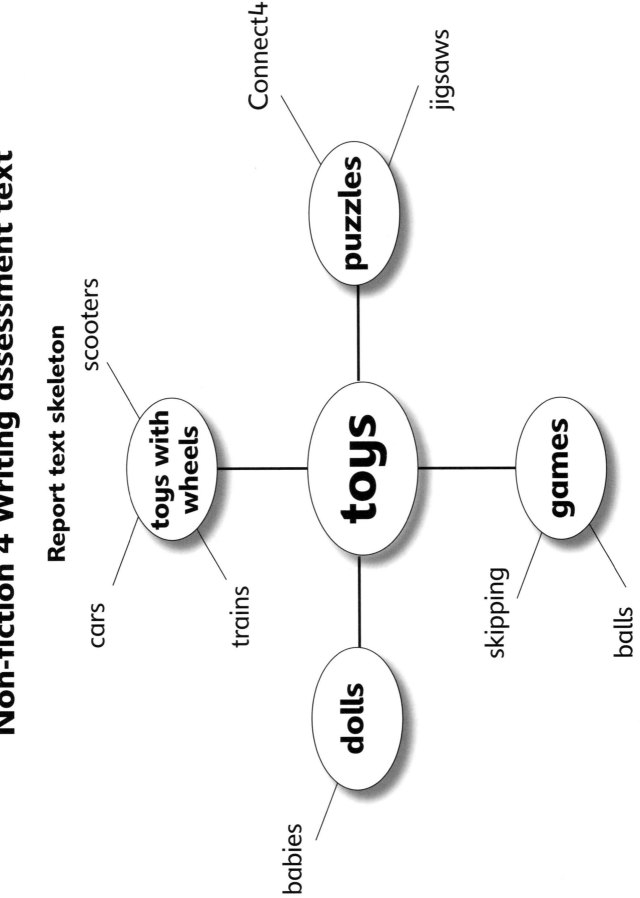

NON-FICTION
UNIT 5 Recount (fact and fiction)

Literacy objectives

Speak and listen for a wide range of purposes in different contexts
Strand 1 Speaking
● Tell stories and describe incidents from their own experience in an audible voice.
Strand 3 Group discussion and interaction
● Explain their views to others in a small group, decide how to report the group's views to the class.

Read and write for a range of purposes on paper and on screen
Strand 5 Word recognition: decoding (reading) and encoding (spelling)
● Recognise and use alternative ways of pronouncing the graphemes already taught.
● Recognise and use alternative ways of spelling the phonemes already taught.
● Identify the constituent parts of two-syllable and three-syllable words to support the application of phonic knowledge and skills.
● Recognise automatically an increasing number of familiar high frequency words.
● Apply phonic knowledge and skills as the prime approach to reading and spelling unfamiliar words that are not completely decodable.
● Read more challenging texts which can be decoded using their acquired phonic knowledge and skills, along with automatic recognition of high frequency words.
● Read and spell phonically decodable two-syllable and three-syllable words.
Strand 6 Word structure and spelling
● Spell new words using phonics as the prime approach.
● Segment sounds into their constituent phonemes in order to spell them correctly.
● Recognise and use alternative ways of spelling the graphemes already taught.
● Use knowledge of common inflections in spelling, such as plurals, -ly, -er.
● Read and spell phonically decodable two-syllable and three-syllable words.
Strand 7 Understanding and interpreting texts
● Identify the main events and characters in stories, and find specific information in simple texts.
● Recognise the main elements that shape different texts.
Strand 9 Creating and shaping texts
● Convey information and ideas in simple non-narrative forms.
● Create short simple texts on paper and screen that combine words with images (and sounds).
Strand 10 Text structure and organisation
● Write chronological and non-chronological texts using simple structures.
Strand 11 Sentence structure and punctuation
● Compose and write simple sentences independently to communicate meaning.
Strand 12 Presentation.
● Use the space bar and keyboard to type their name and simple texts.

Key aspects of learning

Reasoning
● Children will sequence events using visual evidence. Children will be explaining their opinions and returning to the text and their observations to find evidence.

Unit 5 Recount (fact and fiction)

Key aspects of learning (continued)

Evaluation
- Children will discuss success criteria for their written work and begin to judge the effectiveness of their own and others' writing.

Social skills
- When developing collaborative writing, children will learn about assigning roles within a group to complete a task.

Communication
- Children will develop their ability to discuss as they work collaboratively in paired, group and whole-class contexts. They will communicate outcomes orally, in writing and through ICT if appropriate.

Assessment focuses

Reading
AF2 *(understand, describe, select or retrieve information, events or ideas from texts and use quotation and reference to text).*
AF4 *(identify and comment on the structure and organisation of texts, including grammatical and presentational features at text level).*
AF5 *(explain and comment on writers' use of language, including grammatical and literary features at word and sentence level).*

Writing
AF2 *(produce texts which are appropriate to task, reader and purpose).*
AF5 *(vary sentences for clarity, purpose and effect).*
AF6 *(write with technical accuracy of syntax and punctuation in phrases, clauses and sentences).*

Speaking and listening
Speaking (speak with clarity, intonation and pace).
Group discussion and interaction (consider alternatives and reach agreement).

Resources

Phase 1 activities
Photocopiable page, 'Growing sunflowers' (versions 1 and 2)
Interactive activity, 'Recount detectives'
Photocopiable page, 'What type of text?'
Photocopiable page, 'Plant growth' (versions 1 and 2)
Interactive activity, 'Plant growth'
Phase 2 activities
Interactive activity, 'Time connectives'
Photocopiable page, 'Plant growth skeleton' (versions 1 and 2)
Phase 3 activities
Photocopiable page, 'Recount checklist'
Photocopiable page, 'Sentences' (versions 1 and 2)
Periodic assessment
Photocopiable page, 'Non-fiction 5 Reading assessment'
Photocopiable page, 'Non-fiction 5 Writing assessment'

Unit 5 ▣ Recount (fact and fiction)

Learning outcomes	Assessment opportunity and evidence	Assessment focuses (AFs) Level 1	Success criteria
Phase ① activities pages 119-121			
Key features of a recount Children can identify the features of a recount text.	● Supported group activity where children decide if sentences come from a recount text, and then identify the features of a recount by annotating a text. ● Group discussion of the photocopiable activity and independent response to the interactive activity. ● Children's completed photocopiable page, interactive activity and oral responses.	**Reading AF5** Comments on obvious features of language.	I know the key features of recounts.
Recognising a recount Children can identify the features of a recount text.	● Independent and paired activity where children compare two different text extracts to identify the features of a recount and a story text. ● Children's completed photocopiable page and oral responses.	**Reading AF4** Some awareness of meaning of simple text features.	I can recognise a recount.
Sequencing a recount Children can sequence a set of events based on their own experience and observations.	● Paired activity where children sequence a series of pictures to describe the growth of a plant and then note key words relating to the topic. ● Children's written notes on the photocopiable page and oral responses.	**Reading AF4** Some awareness of meaning of simple text features. **Writing AF2** Some indication of basic purpose, particular form or awareness of reader.	I can sequence an event based on what I can see.
Phase ② activity page 122			
Using time connectives Children can orally compose and retell a sequence of events using time connectives to link the sequence.	● Paired activity where children match up connectives to a sequence of pictures. They then rehearse sentences orally and write time connectives onto a skeleton recount frame. ● Discussion of the interactive activity and oral rehearsal of sentences using time connectives. ● Children's completed interactive activity and photocopiable page.	**Writing AF5** ● Reliance on simple phrases and clauses. ● Some sentence-like structures formed by chaining clauses together.	I can write about events using time connectives.

Unit 5 📖 Recount (fact and fiction)

Learning outcomes	Assessment opportunity and evidence	Assessment focuses (AFs)	Success criteria
		Level 1	

Phase ③ activities pages 123-124

Learning outcomes	Assessment opportunity and evidence	Assessment focuses (AFs) Level 1	Success criteria
Group evaluation Children can evaluate a group's plan for a recount.	• Group activity where children evaluate plans for a recount. Notes are made on the photocopiable page and feedback is then given to each group. • Discussion of the recount plans, children's oral feedback and notes on the photocopiable page.	**Reading AF2** • Some simple points from familiar texts recalled. • Some pages/sections of interest located. **Reading AF4** Some awareness of meaning of simple text features.	• I can give feedback on another group's plan. • I can write a plan for a recount.
Sentences Children can write a recount using time connectives to sequence events and correctly demarcate sentences.	• Independent activity where children investigate a series of sentences by ticking those correctly punctuated and then rewriting the incorrect ones using correct punctuation. • Children's completed photocopiable page and oral responses.	**Writing AF6** • Mostly grammatically accurate clauses. • Some awareness of use of full stops and capital letters.	I can write sentences correctly.

Learning outcomes	Assessment opportunity and evidence	Assessment focuses (AFs)		Success criteria
		Level 2	Level 3	

Phase ① activities pages 119-121

Learning outcomes	Assessment opportunity and evidence	Level 2	Level 3	Success criteria
Key features of a recount Children can identify the features of a recount text.	• Independent activity where children decide if sentences come from a recount text, and then identify the features of a recount by annotating a text. • Children's completed photocopiable page, interactive activity and oral responses.	**Reading AF5** • Some effective language choices noted. • Some familiar patterns of language identified.	**Reading AF5** A few basic features of writer's use of language identified, but with little or no comment.	I know the key features of recounts.
Recognising a recount Children can identify the features of a recount text.	• Independent and paired activity where children compare two different text extracts to identify the features of a recount and a story text. • Children's completed photocopiable page and oral responses.	**Reading AF4** Some awareness of use of features of organisation.	**Reading AF4** A few basic features of organisation at text level identified, with little or no linked comment.	I can recognise a recount.

Unit 5 ⬜ Recount (fact and fiction)

Learning outcomes	Assessment opportunity and evidence	Assessment focuses (AFs)		Success criteria
		Level 2	Level 3	
Sequencing a recount Children can sequence a set of events based on their own experience and observations.	• Independent activity where children sequence a series of pictures to describe the growth of a plant and then note key words relating to the topic. • Children's written notes on the photocopiable page and oral responses.	**Reading AF4** Some awareness of use of features of organisation. **Writing AF2** • Some basic purpose established. • Some appropriate features of the given form used. • Some attempts to adopt appropriate style.	**Reading AF4** A few basic features of organisation at text level identified, with little or no linked comment. **Writing AF2** • Purpose established at a general level. • Main features of selected form sometimes signalled to the reader. • Some attempts at appropriate style, with attention to reader.	I can sequence an event based on what I can see.

Phase ② activity page 122

Using time connectives Children can orally compose and retell a sequence of events using time connectives to link the sequence.	• Paired activity where children match up connectives to a sequence of pictures. They then rehearse sentences orally and write time connectives onto a skeleton recount frame. • Discussion of the interactive activity and oral rehearsal of sentences using time connectives. • Children's completed interactive activity, photocopiable page and oral responses.	**Writing AF5** • Some variation in sentence openings. • Mainly simple sentences with *and* used to connect clauses. • Past and present tense generally consistent.	**Writing AF5** • Reliance mainly on simply structured sentences, variation with support. • *and, but, so* are the most common connectives, subordination occasionally. • Some limited variation in use of tense and verb forms, not always secure.	I can write about events using time connectives.

Phase ③ activities pages 123-124

Group evaluation Children can evaluate a group's plan for a recount.	• Group activity where children evaluate plans for a recount. Notes are made on the photocopiable page and feedback is then given to each group. • Discussion of the recount plans, children's oral feedback and notes on the photocopiable page.	**Reading AF2** • Some specific, straightforward information recalled. • Generally clear idea of where to look for information. **Reading AF4** Some awareness of use of features of organisation.	**Reading AF2** • Simple, most obvious points identified though there may also be some misunderstanding. • Some comments include quotations from or references to text, but not always relevant. **Reading AF4** A few basic features of organisation at text level identified, with little or no linked comment.	• I can give feedback on another group's plan. • I can write a plan for a recount.
Sentences Children can write a recount using time connectives to sequence events and correctly demarcate sentences.	• Independent activity where children investigate a series of sentences by ticking those correctly punctuated and then rewriting the incorrect ones using correct punctuation. • Children's completed photocopiable page and oral responses.	**Writing AF6** • Clause structure mostly grammatically correct. • Sentence demarcation with capital letters and full stops usually accurate. • Some accurate use of question and exclamation marks, and commas in lists.	**Writing AF6** • Straightforward sentences usually demarcated accurately with full stops, capital letters, question and exclamation marks. • Some, limited, use of speech punctuation. • Comma splicing evident, particularly in narrative.	I can write sentences correctly.

Phase ① Key features of a recount

Learning outcome
Children can identify the features of a recount text.

Success criteria
I know the key features of recounts.

Setting the context
The children should already be familiar with the key features of a recount text. Display a copy of the photocopiable page 'Growing sunflowers' (version 1 or 2). Read the text together. Explain that each of the pull-out boxes is pointing to a key feature of the text. Hand out a copy of the photocopiable page to each child. Ask them to fill in the boxes by identifying each of the key features.

Assessment opportunity
The children working at level 1 can complete version 1 of the activity in a supported group. When the children have completed the task, ask them to move on to the interactive activity 'Recount detectives'. Explain that some of the features on each screen are not found in a recount text. They should click 'yes' or 'no' to identify the correct and incorrect features.

Assessment evidence
The photocopiable activity will demonstrate the children's knowledge of key features in the context of a written account. The interactive activity highlights their understanding when the text is taken out of context. At level 1, an adult will need to draw out the children's responses with questioning. For example, *What does the first line tell you? How do we know how tall the plant was?* At levels 2–3, the children should be able to identify the features without using a wordbank. Use the completed interactive activity, photocopiable pages and the children's oral responses as evidence against Reading AF5.

Next steps
Support: In a guided reading session, ask the children to identify one specific feature of a recount. Then repeat in future sessions with a different feature.
Extension: Encourage the children to highlight further examples of some of the features in the text.

Key aspects of learning
Reasoning: Children will be explaining their opinions and returning to the text and their observations to find evidence.
Communication: Children will develop their ability to discuss as they work collaboratively in paired, group and whole-class contexts. They will communicate outcomes orally, in writing and through ICT if appropriate.

NON-FICTION

Phase ① Recognising a recount

Learning outcome
Children can identify the features of a recount text.

Success criteria
I can recognise a recount text.

Setting the context
This assessment should be carried out once the children have investigated the key features of a recount text, including the language features that denote a sequence of events ('first', 'then', 'next', 'finally' and so on). They should have also compared recounts with narrative texts and discussed similarities and differences. They will be aware that both can use past-tense verbs and the first person. Display the photocopiable page 'What type of text?' on the whiteboard. Read through the two text extracts together.

Assessment opportunity
Provide the children with their own copies of the photocopiable page and invite them to circle the features that tell them if each text is either a recount or a narrative. Then, ask them to tick their chosen text type underneath each extract. When the children have completed the activity, invite them to swap their pages with a partner and compare the features they each circled. Invite them to explain how the two texts differ. Make notes of their oral responses against the class list.

Assessment evidence
At level 1, the children may recognise that the second text is a story because it contains speech. At levels 2–3, the children will identify the time connectives and glossary in the first extract. The children's oral responses and completed photocopiable pages will provide evidence against Reading AF4.

Next steps
Support: In guided reading sessions, invite the children to collect words from recounts that signal the sequence of events and write them in their personal wordbanks.
Extension: Invite the children to draw up a list of language and layout features that are common to recount texts.

Key aspects of learning
Reasoning: Children will be explaining their opinions and returning to the text and their observations to find evidence.
Communication: Children will develop their ability to discuss as they work collaboratively in paired, group and whole-class contexts. They will communicate outcomes orally, in writing and through ICT if appropriate.

Phase ① Sequencing a recount

Learning outcome
Children can sequence a set of events based on their own experience and observations.

Success criteria
I can sequence an event based on what I can see.

Setting the context
Prior to this assessment, the children should have already completed a science project focusing on growth and change. For example, studying the life cycle of a plant or an animal. Revisit and discuss this previous science work as a whole class. Explain to the children that they are going to be combining what they have learned about writing recounts with the observations they made during their science work. The end goal will be to create their own animated recount.

Assessment opportunity
Provide the children with a copy of the photocopiable page 'Plant growth' (version 1 or 2). Ask them to cut out and sequence the pictures to create the life cycle of a sunflower. (If they wish, they can write a number in each blank circle on the photocopiable to help them organise their pictures.) Then, invite them to make notes of any key words that they think they may need when writing their recount. At level 1, the children can check their sequence with a partner and then collaborate to add notes to version 1 of the photocopiable page.

Assessment evidence
At all levels, the children should be able to sequence the images correctly. When writing notes, the children at level 1 will use simple, descriptive key words. For example, relating to the size or number of leaves. At levels 2–3, the children may add time-related words to their notes. Use the children's oral responses and photocopiable pages to provide evidence against Reading AF4 and Writing AF2.

Next steps
Support: Invite the children to complete the interactive activity 'Plant growth'. They will be presented with four images, which they will need to sequence in the correct order to create the life cycle of a sunflower.
Extension: Mask the pictures on the photocopiable page. Encourage the children to judge if their notes are sufficient to remind them about the event and its sequence.

Key aspects of learning
Reasoning: Children will sequence events using visual evidence.
Communication: Children will develop their ability to discuss as they work collaboratively in paired, group and whole-class contexts. They will communicate outcomes orally, in writing and through ICT if appropriate.

NON-FICTION

Unit 5 ⬜ **Recount (fact and fiction)**

Phase ② Using time connectives

Learning outcome
Children can orally compose and retell a sequence of events using time connectives to link the sequence.

Success criteria
I can write about events using time connectives.

Setting the context
This assessment should be carried out once the children have had experience of using time connectives in modelled writing. They should also have worked in pairs to create their own recount plan using time connectives. Invite the children to do the interactive activity 'Time connectives' with a partner. Explain that they are to match the sentence starters with the images. Encourage them to try out their sentences orally in order to check they have made the best choices.

Assessment opportunity
Listen in as the children rehearse their sentences orally while completing the interactive activity. Afterwards, ask them to change to a new partner and give them a copy of the photocopiable page 'Plant growth skeleton' (version 1 for level 1; version 2 for levels 2–3). Invite them to orally rehearse sentences for each picture in the sequence, before writing a suitable time connective on the page to link each stage. Ask pairs to share their choice of connectives with you and say their sentences aloud. Make notes of their responses against the class list.

Assessment evidence
At level 1, the children will tend to use repetition of 'then' or 'and then' on the photocopiable page. At levels 2–3, the children should demonstrate a more varied choice of connectives. Use the completed interactive activity, photocopiable pages and the children's oral responses to provide evidence against Writing AF5.

Next steps
Support: Ask the children to highlight connecting words in a recount text and then suggest alternatives. Discuss which choice of words works best and why.
Extension: Invite the children to write some of the sentences they rehearsed on the photocopiable page as a paragraph.

Key aspects of learning
Reasoning: Children will sequence events using visual evidence.
Evaluation: Children will discuss success criteria for their written work and begin to judge the effectiveness of their own and others' writing.
Communication: Children will develop their ability to discuss as they work collaboratively in paired, group and whole-class contexts. They will communicate outcomes orally, in writing and through ICT if appropriate.

Phase ③ Group evaluation

Learning outcome
Children can evaluate a group's plan for a recount.

Success criteria
● I can give feedback on another group's plan.
● I can write a plan for a recount.

Setting the context
Prior to this assessment, the children should already be familiar with using stop-frame animation software. In groups, they will have used the software to create their own visual text for their animated recounts (see Phase 1 activity 'Sequencing a recount'). The groups will also have created a plan for their animated visuals and the written text to accompany it. Hold a plenary session and ask the children, in their groups, to look closely at another group's suggested animations and written text plan. Remind the children about the key features of a recount text, which should be included in the final animations. Provide them with the photocopiable page 'Recount checklist'. Explain that each group should make notes on the checklist to help them give feedback.

Assessment opportunity
Invite the groups to give feedback to each other on the proposed plans. This provides an opportunity to assess the children's ability to evaluate another group's work against agreed success criteria and give positive feedback. The feedback should include opinions about whether the sequence is in the correct order, contains enough detail and uses time connectives. This also gives you the opportunity to make notes about the children's plans based on the feedback from the different groups.

Assessment evidence
At level 1, the children will read and make simple comments about the group's plans. For example, 'They use words like next and then'. At levels 2–3, the children will be able to comment on the relevance of the information included and its accuracy. Use the children's notes on the photocopiable pages and oral responses as evidence against Reading AF2 and AF4.

Next steps
Support: Work with groups to improve and extend their plans before they use computers to complete their animations.
Extension: Encourage the children to begin putting their plans into practice.

Key aspects of learning
Reasoning: Children will be explaining their opinions and returning to the text and their observations to find evidence.
Evaluation: Children will discuss success criteria for their written work and begin to judge the effectiveness of their own and others' writing.
Social skills: When developing collaborative writing, children will learn about assigning roles within a group to complete a task.
Communication: Children will develop their ability to discuss as they work collaboratively in paired, group and whole-class contexts. They will communicate outcomes orally, in writing and through ICT if appropriate.

Phase ③ Sentences

Learning outcome
Children can write a recount using time connectives to sequence events and correctly demarcate sentences.

Success criteria
I can write sentences correctly.

Setting the context
This assessment can be undertaken at any time during this phase to ensure that the children understand how to correctly construct a sentence. It will assess whether they can use capital letters, verbs and full stops accurately when writing the captions for their computer animations. Remind the children that a sentence always begins with a capital letter and ends with a full stop. Encourage the children to say what else they know about sentences.

Assessment opportunity
Provide the children with copies of the photocopiable page 'Sentences' (version 1 for those at level 1; version 2 for those at levels 2–3). Explain that there are lines of writing on the page. Some are written as correct sentences and some have errors. Invite the children to tick the correct sentences and rewrite the others correctly. Afterwards, invite the children to describe to you what needed correcting in the sentences that they wrote.

Assessment evidence
This activity provides an opportunity to assess the children's security in writing and punctuating sentences to ensure the text for their animated recounts is correctly written. At level 1, the children may fail to spot the incorrect use of the upper-case 'S' in the second sentence. Use the completed photocopiable pages and children's oral responses as evidence against Writing AF6.

Next steps
Support: Use guided writing sessions to work with the children to improve their punctuation.
Extension: Invite the children to work with a partner to check each other's sentences.

Key aspects of learning
Evaluation: Children will discuss success criteria for their written work and begin to judge the effectiveness of their own and others' writing.
Communication: Children will develop their ability to discuss as they work collaboratively in paired, group and whole-class contexts. They will communicate outcomes orally, in writing and through ICT if appropriate.

Periodic assessment

Reading

Learning outcome
Children can sequence a set of events based on their own experience and observations.

Success criteria
- I can sequence an event based on observations.
- I can read two-syllable and three-syllable words.

Setting the context
Ensure the children have already had experience of reading personal recount texts in shared and guided reading. Review the work that has been done during the course of this unit and discuss the children's achievements with them. Ask them what they found easy and what they found difficult.

Assessment opportunity
Provide the children with a copy of the photocopiable page 'Non-fiction 5 Reading assessment'. Invite them to cut out the cards and group them according to their number of syllables. Then, ask them to use each word in a sentence, saying it aloud to a partner. At level 1, the children can complete this activity in a supported group. Make notes of individual children's oral responses against the class list.

Assessment evidence
The children's oral responses and evidence collected during the course of the unit will provide evidence against Reading AF1.

Writing

Learning outcome
Children can write a recount using time connectives to sequence events and correctly demarcate sentences.

Success criteria
- I can write a recount text using time connectives.
- I can use the computer to write a recount text.

Setting the context
Show the group's completed animated recounts to the class. Discuss what worked well and what could be improved upon. Ask the children to say what they found easy or difficult about the work in this unit. How well did they work together as a group? What did they find most enjoyable?

Assessment opportunity
Invite the children to write their own review of their presentation. Explain that they should write a brief introduction and then describe what they found hard and what they found easy to accomplish. They should then go on to write about what they enjoyed, what they could add to their presentation and what they think could be changed. If necessary, the children can be given copies of the photocopiable page 'Non-fiction 5 Writing assessment' to structure their responses using the grid. If possible, show the children's presentations to another class in the school and ask them to give feedback.

Assessment evidence
At level 1, the children can write their review in a supported group, using the grid on the photocopiable page. Make comparisons between your own assessment of the children's writing during this unit and the oral responses of their own achievements and written reviews. This can be used to provide evidence against Writing AF3.

NON-FICTION

Name	Date

What type of text?

- Read both of these texts.
- Circle the features that tell you what type of text it is.
- Tick the text type.

Last May I saw a swan with seven cygnets on the river. They had light grey feathers called down.

I saw them next in June. The cygnets were now about half as big as the mother swan.

Then I saw them again in September. The cygnets had grown. Their feathers were nearly white.

cygnet – baby swan
down – the first fluffy feathers of a baby bird

Mark ran down to the river. He wanted to see the baby swans. Mark stood very still and waited. Then he saw seven, tiny, fluffy cygnets on the river.

"Oh, they are so cute!" he said. "I want one as a pet. I will call it Sid!"

When Mark got home he told his mum about the cygnets.

"They are wild birds," she said. "They need to be free on the river."

"Can I go and see them again?" he asked.

"Yes, but don't go too near. You might scare them away."

non-fiction recount ☐   **non-fiction recount** ☐

story ☐   **story** ☐

Red
Amber
Green

I can recognise a recount text. ☐

Name   Date

Plant growth skeleton (1)

- Use connectives to say a sentence for each picture.
- Write a time connective above each arrow to link the pictures in the skeleton.

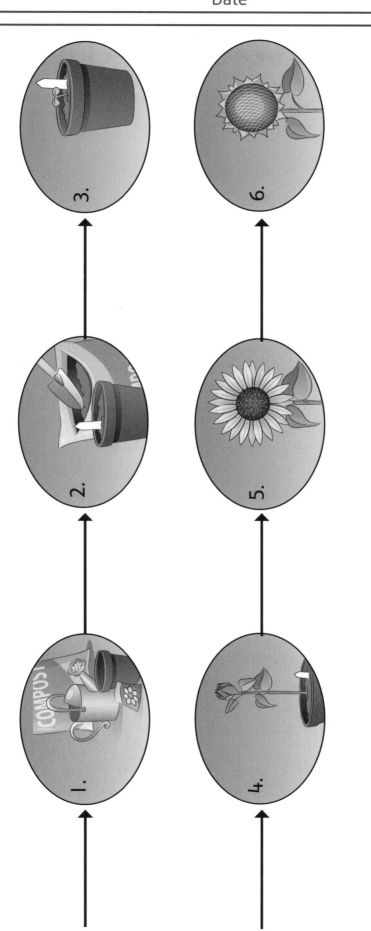

I can write about events using time connectives. ☐

Red
Amber
Green

Illustration © 2010, Anna Godwin/The Illustrator Agency.

NON-FICTION

Name   Date

Recount checklist

◢ Make notes on the checklist about the animation plan.

1. **Introduction:** Does it set the scene – who, what, when, where, how?

_____

_____

2. **Sequence of events:** Is it in the right order? Has anything been missed out?

_____

_____

3. **Details:** Does it have interesting details? Does it need more detail?

_____

_____

4. **Words:** Does it use time connectives? Is it in the past tense? Does it have factual description?

_____

_____

Red
Amber   I can give feedback on another group's plan. ☐
Green

Name   Date

Sentences (1)

■ Find the two correct sentences and tick their boxes.
Then rewrite the incorrect sentences in the spaces below.

1. We filled a pot with soil.   ☐

_____

2. I put a seed into the soil   ☐

_____

3. The seed grew a shoot.   ☐

_____

4. The shoot grew tall.   ☐

_____

Red
Amber   I can write sentences correctly. ☐
Green

POETRY
UNIT 1 Using the senses

Literacy objectives

Speak and listen for a wide range of purposes in different contexts
Strand 1 Speaking
● Interpret a text by reading aloud with some variety in pace and emphasis.
Strand 2 Listening and responding
● Listen with sustained concentration, building new stores of words in different contexts.

Read and write for a range of purposes on paper and on screen
Strand 5 Word recognition: decoding (reading) and encoding (spelling)
● Recognise and use alternative ways of pronouncing the graphemes already taught.
● Recognise and use alternative ways of spelling the phonemes already taught.
● Identify the constituent parts of two-syllable and three-syllable words to support the application of phonic knowledge and skills.
● Recognise automatically an increasing number of familiar high frequency words.
● Apply phonic knowledge and skills as the prime approach to reading and spelling unfamiliar words that are not completely decodable.
● Read more challenging texts which can be decoded using their acquired phonic knowledge and skills, along with automatic recognition of high frequency words.
● Read and spell phonically decodable two-syllable and three-syllable words.
Strand 6 Word structure and spelling
● Spell new words using phonics as the prime approach.
● Segment sounds into their constituent phonemes in order to spell them correctly.
● Recognise and use alternative ways of spelling the graphemes already taught.
● Use knowledge of common inflections in spelling, such as plurals, -ly, -er.
● Read and spell phonically decodable two-syllable and three-syllable words.
Strand 7 Understanding and interpreting texts
● Explore the effect of patterns of language and repeated words and phrases.
Strand 8 Engaging with and responding to texts
● Visualise and comment on events, characters and ideas, making imaginative links to their own experiences.
Strand 9 Creating and shaping texts
● Find and use new and interesting words and phrases, including story language.
● Create short simple texts on paper and screen that combine words with images (and sounds).
Strand 12 Presentation
● Write most letters, correctly formed and orientated, using a comfortable and efficient pencil grip.
● Write with spaces between words accurately.
● Use the space bar and keyboard to type their name and simple texts.

Key aspects of learning

Enquiry
● Children will play games and ask questions about what they can see, hear, feel (touch), smell and taste.

Unit 1 ☐ Using the senses

POETRY

Key aspects of learning (continued)

Reasoning
- Children will explain the words they and others chose to describe objects and experiences.

Evaluation
- Children will discuss success criteria for describing objects and experiences, give feedback to others and judge the effectiveness of their word choices.

Empathy and self-awareness
- Children will hear or read about the sensory experience (and emotional reaction) of others and compare it to their own.

Communication
- Children will begin to develop their ability to discuss the language of poetry and to communicate their own observations and experiences through carefully chosen words. They will sometimes work collaboratively in pairs and groups. They will communicate outcomes orally, and in writing (possibly including ICT).

Assessment focuses

Reading
AF1 (use a range of strategies, including accurate decoding of text, to read for meaning).
AF5 (explain and comment on writers' use of language, including grammatical and literary features at word and sentence level).

Writing
AF1 (write imaginative, interesting and thoughtful texts).
AF7 (select appropriate and effective vocabulary).

Speaking and listening
Speaking (speak with clarity, intonation and pace).
Listening and responding (listen with sustained concentration).

Resources

Phase 1 activities
Interactive activity, 'The senses'
Photocopiable page, 'Sound, taste, touch'
Photocopiable page, 'Sight and smell'
Photocopiable page, 'These are the hands'
Phase 2 activities
Photocopiable page, 'What is it?'
Phase 3 activities
Image, 'Street market'
Interactive activity, 'Identifying the senses'
Photocopiable page, 'Describing the scene' (versions 1 and 2)
Phase 4 activities
Photocopiable page, 'Senses poem'
Periodic assessment
Interactive activity, 'Poetry 1 Reading assessment'
Photocopiable page, 'Poetry 1 Writing assessment'

Unit 1 ▢ Using the senses

Learning outcomes	Assessment opportunity and evidence	Assessment focuses (AFs)		Success criteria
		Level 1		

Phase ① activities pages 135-137

Learning outcomes	Assessment opportunity and evidence	Assessment focuses (AFs) / Level 1	Success criteria
Sound, touch, taste Children can listen to poems and identify words and phrases that describe what we see, hear, feel (touch), smell and taste.	• Independent and paired activity where children classify words based on the senses and then complete a sense spidergram by adding words to describe sound, touch and taste. • Discussion and sharing of word choices. • Children's completed interactive activity, photocopiable page and oral responses.	**Reading AF5** Comments on obvious features of language.	I can listen to poems and find words that describe what we can hear, feel and taste.
Sights and smells Children can listen to poems and identify words and phrases that describe what we see, hear, feel (touch), smell and taste.	• Group and independent activity where children experience a collection of sights and smells and use words from their own experience to describe them. • Children's completed photocopiable page and oral responses.	**Writing AF7** • Mostly simple vocabulary. • Communicates meaning through repetition of key words.	I can listen to poems and find words that describe what we can see and smell.
Actions Children can recite poems in unison, following the rhythm and keeping time, inventing actions where appropriate.	• Supported group activity where children rehearse and perform an action poem. • Discussion, rehearsal and performance of the action poem. • Children's group evaluations and oral responses.	**Reading AF1** • Some high frequency and familiar words read fluently and automatically. • Decode familiar and some unfamiliar words using blending as the prime approach. • Some awareness of punctuation marks.	• I can read a poem with others. • I can invent actions for a poem with others.

Phase ② activity page 138

Learning outcomes	Assessment opportunity and evidence	Assessment focuses (AFs) / Level 1	Success criteria
What is it? Children can identify details of their sensory experience and start to select suitable words and phrases to describe these.	• Paired activity where children describe a picture of an object using sensory vocabulary and their partner must guess what it is. • Discussion and use of sensory vocabulary. • Children's peer-evaluations and oral responses.	**Writing AF1** • Basic information and ideas conveyed through appropriate word choice. • Some descriptive language.	I can describe objects and events using the senses.

Unit 1 — Using the senses

Learning outcomes	Assessment opportunity and evidence	Assessment focuses (AFs)	Success criteria
		Level 1	
Phase ③ activity page 139			
Street market Children can identify details of their sensory responses to images and start to select suitable words and phrases to describe these.	• Paired activity where children describe an image by selecting the most appropriate sensory descriptions using dictionaries and wordbanks to help them. • Discussion and evaluation of word choices. • Children's completed interactive activity, photocopiable page and oral responses.	**Writing AF1** • Basic information and ideas conveyed through appropriate word choice. • Some descriptive language.	I can write about objects and events using the senses.
Phase ④ activity page 140			
Sensory poems Children can identify detailed sensory responses to direct experience and start to select and write suitable words and phrases to describe these.	• Paired activity where children write a poem about an experience using a writing frame and then read it to the class for feedback. • Discussion and sharing of wordbanks. • Children's completed photocopiable page, oral responses and peer feedback.	**Writing AF7** • Mostly simple vocabulary. • Communicates meaning through repetition of key words.	I can write about an experience using the senses.

Learning outcomes	Assessment opportunity and evidence	Assessment focuses (AFs)		Success criteria
		Level 2	Level 3	
Phase ① activities pages 135–137				
Sound, touch, taste Children can listen to poems and identify words and phrases that describe what we see, hear, feel (touch), smell and taste.	• Independent and paired activity where children classify words based on the senses and then complete a sense spidergram by adding words to describe sound, touch and taste. • Paired discussion and sharing of word choices. • Children's completed interactive activity, photocopiable page and oral responses.	**Reading AF5** • Some effective language choices noted. • Some familiar patterns of language identified.	**Reading AF5** A few basic features of writer's use of language identified, but with little or no comment.	I can listen to poems and find words that describe what we can hear, feel and taste.
Sights and smells Children can listen to poems and identify words and phrases that describe what we see, hear, feel (touch), smell and taste.	• Group and independent activity where children experience a collection of sights and smells and use words from their own experience to describe them. • Children's completed photocopiable page and oral responses.	**Writing AF7** • Simple, often speech-like vocabulary conveys relevant meanings. • Some adventurous word choices.	**Writing AF7** • Simple, generally appropriate vocabulary used, limited in range. • Some words selected for effect or occasion.	I can listen to poems and find words that describe what we can see and smell.

POETRY

Learning outcomes	Assessment opportunity and evidence	Assessment focuses (AFs)		Success criteria
		Level 2	**Level 3**	
Actions Children can recite poems in unison, following the rhythm and keeping time, inventing actions where appropriate.	● Group activity where children rehearse and perform an action poem. ● Discussion, rehearsal and performance of the action poem. ● Children's group evaluations and oral responses.	**Reading AF1** ● Range of key words read on sight. ● Unfamiliar words decoded using appropriate strategies. ● Some fluency and expression.	**Reading AF1** Range of strategies used mostly effectively to read with fluency, understanding and expression.	● I can read a poem with others. ● I can invent actions for a poem with others.

Phase ② activity page 138

What is it? Children can identify details of their sensory experience and start to select suitable words and phrases to describe these.	● Paired activity where children describe a picture of an object using sensory vocabulary and their partner must guess what it is. ● Discussion and use of sensory vocabulary. ● Children's peer-evaluations and oral responses.	**Writing AF1** ● Mostly relevant ideas and content, sometimes repetitive or sparse. ● Some apt word choices create interest. ● Brief comments, questions about events or actions suggest viewpoint.	**Writing AF1** ● Some appropriate ideas and content included. ● Some attempt to elaborate on basic information or events. ● Attempt to adopt viewpoint, though often not maintained or inconsistent.	I can describe objects and events using the senses.

Phase ③ activity page 139

Street market Children can identify details of their sensory responses to images and start to select suitable words and phrases to describe these.	● Independent and paired activity where children describe an image by selecting the most appropriate sensory descriptions using dictionaries and wordbanks to help them. ● Discussion and evaluation of word choices. ● Children's completed interactive activity, photocopiable page and oral responses.	**Writing AF1** ● Mostly relevant ideas and content, sometimes repetitive or sparse. ● Some apt word choices create interest. ● Brief comments, questions about events or actions suggest viewpoint.	**Writing AF1** ● Some appropriate ideas and content included. ● Some attempt to elaborate on basic information or events. ● Attempt to adopt viewpoint, though often not maintained or inconsistent.	I can write about objects and events using the senses.

Phase ④ activity page 140

Sensory poems Children can identify detailed sensory responses to direct experience and start to select and write suitable words and phrases to describe these.	● Independent activity where children write a poem about an experience using a writing frame and then read it to the class for feedback. ● Children's completed photocopiable page, oral responses and peer feedback.	**Writing AF7** ● Simple, often speech-like vocabulary conveys relevant meanings. ● Some adventurous word choices.	**Writing AF7** ● Simple, generally appropriate vocabulary used, limited in range. ● Some words selected for effect or occasion.	I can write about an experience using the senses.

📖 SCHOLASTIC

Phase ① Sound, touch, taste

Learning outcome

Children can listen to poems and identify words and phrases that describe what we see, hear, feel (touch), smell and taste.

Success criteria

I can listen to poems and find words that describe what we can hear, feel and taste.

Setting the context

Prior to this assessment, the children should have listened to and joined in with poems about the senses. They will have explored rhythm in poetry and practised keeping time by clapping, walking, marching or similar activities. They should also have explored what is meant by the five senses and identified words in poems that are used to describe them.

Assessment opportunity

Invite the children to complete the interactive activity 'The senses'. Explain that they are to classify words about the senses by dragging them into the correct category. When they have completed the activity, provide them with the photocopiable page 'Sound, taste, touch'. In pairs, ask them to add words to each sense spidergram by recalling words from the interactive activity and from their own knowledge. Explain that some words may be used for more than one sense. For example, 'soft' could relate to touch but also to sound. Afterwards, hold a plenary session to compare the words that the children chose. Ask them if they can recall any poems read in the unit that have included any of their words. Which words do they enjoy the sounds of most? Make notes of oral responses against the class list.

Assessment evidence

At level 1, the children will recall single words to describe the senses. For example, remembering the word 'slurp' as a sound word in a poem. At levels 2–3, the children may recall words as adjectives or rhyming phrases. The completed interactive activity, photocopiable pages and children's oral responses will provide evidence against Reading AF5.

Next steps

Support: Focus on one sense at a time during guided reading sessions and help the children identify the words related to that one sense.
Extension: Encourage the children to add phrases to the spidergram. For example, pairs of rhymes or alliteration.

Key aspects of learning

Reasoning: Children will explain the words they and others chose to describe objects and experiences.
Communication: Children will begin to develop their ability to discuss the language of poetry and to communicate their own observations and experiences through carefully chosen words. They will sometimes work collaboratively in pairs and groups. They will communicate outcomes orally, and in writing (possibly including ICT).

Phase ① Sights and smells

Learning outcome
Children can listen to poems and identify words and phrases that describe what we see, hear, feel (touch), smell and taste.

Success criteria
I can listen to poems and find words that describe what we can see and smell.

Setting the context
The children should have already completed the previous assessment activity. Explain that they are going to focus on two senses: sight and smell. Provide the class with a sensory experience by arranging two displays - one for each sense. The smell display could feature scented oils, foods, perfumes, flowers and so on. The sight display could feature different objects and materials that have strong shapes, textures or reflective properties. In groups, invite the children to explore the displays without touching anything. On a sheet of paper, ask them to write down any words they can think of to describe what they can see on the sight display or smell on the smell display.

Assessment opportunity
Once the groups have explored each display, ask them to add the words that they have written to the spidergram on the photocopiable page 'Sight and smell'. The children should work independently on this task. Hold a plenary session and compare the words the children added to their spidergrams. Ask them if they can recall any poems read in the unit that have included any of their words. Which words do they enjoy the sounds of most? Make notes of their oral responses against the class list.

Assessment evidence
At level 1, the children will describe smells by using words that express their opinion. For example, 'bad' or 'nice'. For the sight display, they will focus on words to describe colour or shape. At levels 2-3, the children will provide more adventurous word choices. For example, they may describe the smells as 'strong', 'flowery' or 'sweet'. The completed photocopiable pages and children's oral responses will provide evidence against Writing AF7.

Next steps
Support: Use guided reading opportunities to help the children build up their personal wordbanks with sensory words and descriptions.
Extension: Select sensory poems for the children to read independently.

Key aspects of learning
Enquiry: Children will play games and ask questions about what they can see, hear, feel (touch), smell and taste.
Reasoning: Children will explain the words they chose to describe objects and experiences.
Empathy and self-awareness: Children will hear or read about the sensory experience (and emotional reaction) of others and compare it to their own.
Communication: Children will begin to develop their ability to discuss the language of poetry and to communicate their own observations and experiences through carefully chosen words. They will sometimes work collaboratively in pairs and groups. They will communicate outcomes orally, and in writing (possibly including ICT).

Phase ① Actions

Learning outcome

Children can recite poems in unison, following the rhythm and keeping time, inventing actions where appropriate.

Success criteria
- I can read a poem with others.
- I can invent actions for a poem with others.

Setting the context
Prior to this assessment, the children should have had opportunities to practise and read poems in unison, following a rhythm and keeping time. They should also have invented actions to be performed when reading or reciting poems. Arrange the children into small ability groups, with children at level 1 working with a supporting adult. Provide them with copies of the poem 'These are the hands' by Paul Cookson (on the photocopiable page). Invite the children to read the poem together and work out actions to suit each line. Allocate one or two verses to each group and allow them sufficient time to rehearse reading the verses in unison.

Assessment opportunity
Hold a plenary session and work round the groups, asking each in turn to stand and read one verse together with actions. Encourage the groups to comment on each other's reading and actions. Make notes of the children's oral contributions against the class list.

Assessment evidence
At level 1, the children should be able to say the repeated lines from memory and use phonics to decode the last words in the lines. At levels 2-3, the children will read the poem fluently and with expression. Use observations and the children's oral responses to provide evidence against Reading AF1.

Next steps
Support: Work with small groups during guided reading sessions, to practise reading in unison.
Extension: In groups, encourage the children to practise a choral performance of the whole poem.

Key aspects of learning
Evaluation: Children will discuss success criteria for describing objects and experiences, give feedback to others and judge the effectiveness of their word choices.
Empathy and self-awareness: Children will hear or read about the sensory experience (and emotional reaction) of others and compare it to their own.
Communication: Children will begin to develop their ability to discuss the language of poetry and to communicate their own observations and experiences through carefully chosen words. They will sometimes work collaboratively in pairs and groups. They will communicate outcomes orally, and in writing (possibly including ICT).

POETRY

Phase ② What is it?

Learning outcome
Children can identify details of their sensory experience and start to select suitable words and phrases to describe these.

Success criteria
I can describe objects and events using the senses.

Setting the context
This assessment should be carried out once the children have played a range of games to explore their senses. For example, identifying familiar objects inside a feely bag, blindfold tasting, identifying mystery sounds and so on. They should also have begun to identify details of sensory observations and found simple words and phrases to describe these. In pairs, provide the children with copies of the photocopiable page 'What is it?'. Ask them to cut out the picture cards and divide them between themselves. The children should then take turns to choose a picture card and describe what is on it by saying what it feels, looks, sounds, smells or tastes like. Their partner has to guess what is being described.

Assessment opportunity
Invite the children to feed back about their partner's choice of sensory words to describe the pictures. Did their partner use words relating to more than one sense for each picture? Could they make an informed guess about the object on the picture? Make notes of the children's responses against the class list.

Assessment evidence
At level 1, the children will use simple adjectives that mostly relate to appearance. At levels 2-3, the children will begin to use similes to describe the pictures and include other senses such as touch and sound. Use the children's oral responses and notes made against the class list to provide evidence against Writing AF1.

Next steps
Support: Display a selection of cards and describe one of them to a small group, challenging them to pick out the correct card. Repeat the game, letting each child take a turn.
Extension: Challenge the children to describe their pictures using all five senses.

Key aspects of learning
Enquiry: Children will play games and ask questions about what they can see, hear, feel (touch), smell and taste.
Reasoning: Children will explain the words they and others chose to describe objects and experiences.
Evaluation: Children will discuss success criteria for describing objects and experiences, give feedback to others and judge the effectiveness of their word choices.
Empathy and self-awareness: Children will hear or read about the sensory experience (and emotional reaction) of others and compare it to their own.
Communication: Children will begin to develop their ability to discuss the language of poetry and to communicate their own observations and experiences through carefully chosen words. They will sometimes work collaboratively in pairs and groups. They will communicate outcomes orally, and in writing (possibly including ICT).

Phase ③ Street market

Learning outcome
Children can identify details of their sensory responses to images and start to select suitable words and phrases to describe these.

Success criteria
I can write about objects and events using the senses.

Setting the context
Prior to this assessment, the children should have discussed objects, scenes and events by describing what they can see, as well as what they think they might be able to feel, hear, smell and taste if they were actually there. They should also have had the opportunity to use a dictionary or wordbank to help them find words and improve their vocabulary. Give the children copies of the image 'Street market' and display the interactive activity 'Identifying the senses'. Explain to the children that they should complete the interactive activity using the image to help them.

Assessment opportunity
At level 1, the children can work on the activity with a partner. Those at levels 2–3 work independently. Afterwards, put the children into pairs and provide them with the photocopiable page 'Describing the scene' (version 1 for those at level 1; version 2 for those at levels 2–3). Encourage them to make use of a dictionary and any wordbanks that they have created to help them describe the scene. Afterwards, ask pairs to read out their words and give reasons for their choices. Invite them to compare their choices with another pair, to evaluate each other's work.

Assessment evidence
At level 1, the children will focus mainly on adjectives related to sight. At levels 2–3, the children will use more adventurous vocabulary, including words related to smell and sound. Use the children's oral responses, completed interactive activity and photocopiable pages to provide evidence against Writing AF1.

Next steps
Support: Work with the children to describe other images using the five senses.
Extension: Encourage the children to use their words to create a simple poem describing the market scene.

Key aspects of learning
Enquiry: Children will play games and ask questions about what they can see, hear, feel (touch), smell and taste.
Reasoning: Children will explain the words they and others chose to describe objects and experiences.
Evaluation: Children will discuss success criteria for describing objects and experiences, give feedback to others and judge the effectiveness of their word choices.
Empathy and self-awareness: Children will hear or read about the sensory experience (and emotional reaction) of others and compare it to their own.
Communication: Children will begin to develop their ability to discuss the language of poetry and to communicate their own observations and experiences through carefully chosen words. They will sometimes work collaboratively in pairs and groups. They will communicate outcomes orally, and in writing (possibly including ICT).

POETRY

Phase ④ Sensory poems

Learning outcome
Children can identify detailed sensory responses to direct experience and start to select and write suitable words and phrases to describe these.

Success criteria
I can write about an experience using the senses.

Setting the context
Prior to this assessment, the children should have already recalled and explored a familiar or special experience using the senses. They should have generated and discussed effective words for describing the experience and had an opportunity to use their vocabulary in modelled-writing sessions. Remind the children of one of the experiences that you have explored. Explain that they are going to re-use their collections of effective words to write a poem about the experience.

Assessment opportunity
Provide the children with copies of the photocopiable writing frame 'Senses poem'. Ask the children to add two lines to each verse of the poem using effective words relating to each sense (the first line of each verse is given). The children working at level 1 can work with a partner and share their collections of effective words. Afterwards, invite the children to share their poems with the class. Encourage the audience to respond to each poem by finding two examples that they think worked well and one thing that could be improved.

Assessment evidence
At level 1, the children will tend to use simple vocabulary with limited use of adjectives. At levels 2–3, the children will make attempts to use more varied and adventurous language. Use the completed poems and the children's oral responses to provide evidence against Writing AF7.

Next steps
Support: The children can work in a group with a supporting adult to improve their poems.
Extension: Encourage the children to read each other's poems and decide how to order them for a class anthology.

Key aspects of learning
Reasoning: Children will explain the words they and others chose to describe objects and experiences.
Evaluation: Children will discuss success criteria for describing objects and experiences, give feedback to others and judge the effectiveness of their word choices.
Empathy and self-awareness: Children will hear or read about the sensory experience (and emotional reaction) of others and compare it to their own.
Communication: Children will begin to develop their ability to discuss the language of poetry and to communicate their own observations and experiences through carefully chosen words. They will sometimes work collaboratively in pairs and groups. They will communicate outcomes orally, and in writing (possibly including ICT).

Periodic assessment

Reading

Learning outcome
Children can listen to poems and identify words and phrases that describe what we see, hear, feel (touch), smell and taste.

Success criteria
I can listen to poems and find words that describe what we can see, hear, feel, smell and taste.

Setting the context
Review the poetry that the children have read during the course of this unit and ask them to comment on their favourites, giving reasons for their choices. Encourage them to identify particular words and phrases in the poems that refer to the senses. Make notes of their responses against the class list.

Assessment opportunity
Invite the children to complete the interactive activity 'Poetry 1 Reading assessment'. This task provides an opportunity to assess the children's ability to read and understand words and phrases that relate to each of the five senses.

Assessment evidence
The children's completed interactive activity and notes made against the class list can be used to provide evidence against Reading AF1 and AF5.

Writing

Learning outcome
Children can identify detailed sensory responses to direct experience and start to select and write suitable words and phrases to describe these.

Success criteria
- I can write about an experience using the senses.
- I can say why I like a poem about the senses.

Setting the context
Collect the work that has been completed during the course of this unit and discuss the children's achievements with them, individually. Ask them to suggest what they found difficult about the work in the unit and what they found easy to accomplish. Ask the children to choose their favourite piece of written work from the unit. It could be a piece that was completed as part of a group or shared writing task.

Assessment opportunity
Provide the children with a copy of the photocopiable page 'Poetry 1 Writing assessment'. Invite them to explain why they chose the poem and to identify the language used in the poem to describe the senses. This activity provides an opportunity to assess the children's ability to evaluate their own poetry writing and to give reasons for their opinion.

Assessment evidence
At level 1, the children will use simple descriptive language using colour and shape adjectives and simple 'feeling' adjectives such as 'cold' or 'wet'. At levels 2–3, the children will begin to use more imaginative descriptions such as 'frozen' or 'soaked'. Use the children's completed photocopiable pages and work done throughout the unit to provide evidence against Writing AF1.

Name   Date

POETRY

Sound, taste, touch

- Complete each spidergram by adding words that describe each sense.

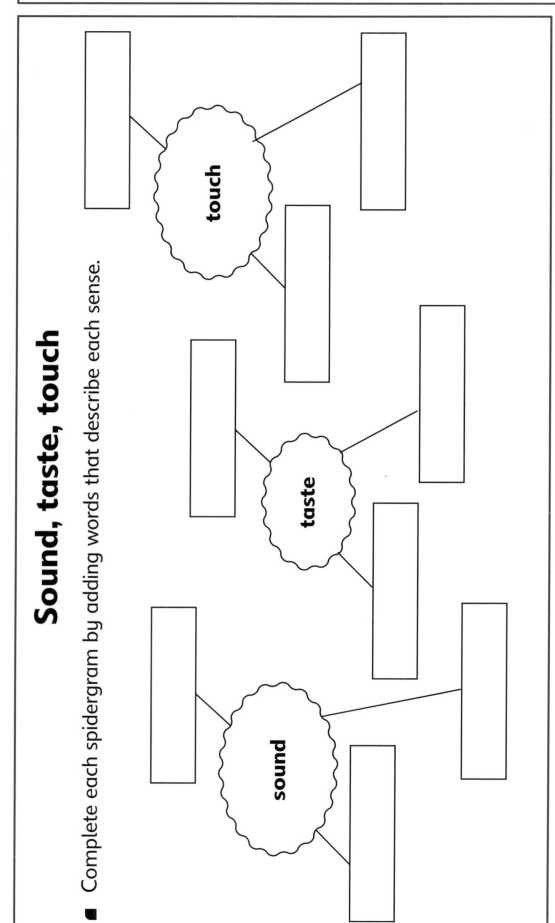

I can listen to poems and find words that describe what we can hear, feel and taste.

Red
Amber
Green

These are the hands

These are the hands that wave
These are the hands that clap
These are the hands that pray
These are the hands that tap

These are the hands that grip
These are the hands that write
These are the hands that paint
These are the hands that fight

These are the hands that hug
These are the hands that squeeze
These are the hands that point
These are the hands that tease

These are the hands that fix
These are the hands that mend
These are the hands that give
These are the hands that lend

These are the hands that take
These are the hands that poke
These are the hands that heal
These are the hands that stroke

These are the hands that hold
These are the hands that love
These are the hands of mine
That fit me like a glove.

Paul Cookson

Text © 2007, Paul Cookson. Illustration © 2010, Simon Smith/Beehive Illustration.

Name   Date

Senses poem

This is what I remember seeing

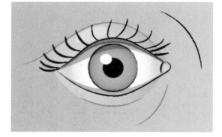

_____

_____

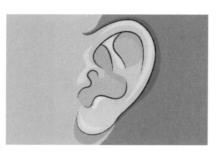

This is what I remember hearing

_____

_____

This is what I remember feeling

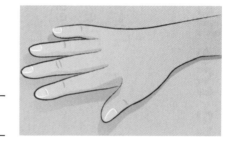

_____

_____

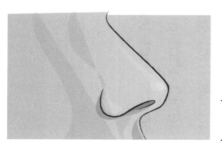

This is what I remember smelling

_____

_____

This is what I remember tasting

_____

_____

Red
Amber
Green

I can write about an experience using the senses.

POETRY

Illustrations © 2010, Anna Godwin/The Illustrator Agency.

Name _____ Date _____

Poetry 1 Writing assessment

My favourite poem

The poem is called:_____

_____

The poem was written by: _____

The poem is about:_____

_____

_____

Words I like in the poem

```
┌──────────────────────────────────────────────┐
│                                                │
│                                                │
│                                                │
│                                                │
└──────────────────────────────────────────────┘
```

I chose this poem because:_____

_____

_____

_____

Red
Amber
Green

I can write about an experience using the senses. ☐
I can say why I like a poem about the senses. ☐

POETRY
UNIT 2 Pattern and rhyme

Literacy objectives

Speak and listen for a wide range of purposes in different contexts
Strand 1 Speaking
- Interpret a text by reading aloud with some variety in pace and emphasis.

Strand 2 Listening and responding
- Listen with sustained concentration, building new stores of words in different contexts.

Strand 3 Group discussion and interaction
- Ask and answer questions, make relevant contributions, offer suggestions and take turns.
- Explain their views to others in a small group, decide how to report the group's views to the class.

Read and write for a range of purposes on paper and on screen
Strand 5 Word recognition: decoding (reading) and encoding (spelling)
- Recognise and use alternative ways of pronouncing the graphemes already taught.
- Recognise and use alternative ways of spelling the phonemes already taught.
- Identify the constituent parts of two-syllable and three-syllable words to support the application of phonic knowledge and skills.
- Recognise automatically an increasing number of familiar high frequency words.
- Apply phonic knowledge and skills as the prime approach to reading and spelling unfamiliar words that are not completely decodable.
- Read more challenging texts which can be decoded using their acquired phonic knowledge and skills, along with automatic recognition of high frequency words.
- Read and spell phonically decodable two-syllable and three-syllable words.

Strand 6 Word structure and spelling
- Spell new words using phonics as the prime approach.
- Segment sounds into their constituent phonemes in order to spell them correctly.
- Recognise and use alternative ways of spelling the graphemes already taught.
- Use knowledge of common inflections in spelling, such as plurals, -ly, -er.
- Read and spell phonically decodable two-syllable and three-syllable words.

Strand 7 Understanding and interpreting texts
- Explore the effect of patterns of language and repeated words and phrases.

Strand 8 Engaging with and responding to texts
- Visualise and comment on events, characters and ideas, making imaginative links to their own experiences.

Strand 9 Creating and shaping texts
- Find and use new and interesting words and phrases, including story language.
- Create short simple texts on paper and screen that combine words with images (and sounds).

Strand 12 Presentation
- Write most letters, correctly formed and orientated, using a comfortable and efficient pencil grip.
- Write with spaces between words accurately.

Key aspects of learning

Enquiry
● Children will hear, read and respond to rhymes and simple, patterned stories, exploring the patterns created by words and phrases.
Reasoning
● Children will explain the words they and others chose to complete their compositions.
Evaluation
● Children will record their composition on audio or video as a vehicle for review.
Empathy and self-awareness
● Children will hear the patterns created by others and discuss their views – giving positive and constructive feedback.
Communication
● Children will begin to develop their ability to discuss the language of poetry and to communicate through carefully chosen words. They will sometimes work collaboratively in pairs and groups. They will communicate outcomes orally, and in writing (possibly including ICT).

Assessment focuses

Reading
AF1 (use a range of strategies, including accurate decoding of text, to read for meaning).
AF5 (explain and comment on writers' use of language, including grammatical and literary features at word and sentence level).

Writing
AF7 (select appropriate and effective vocabulary).

Speaking and listening
Speaking (speak with clarity, intonation and pace).
Listening and responding (listen with sustained concentration).
Group discussion and interaction (listen to each other's views and preferences, agree the next steps to take and identify contributions by each group member).

Resources

Phase 1 activities
Photocopiable page, 'Five Little Speckled Frogs'
Interactive activity, 'Rhymes and patterns'
Phase 2 activities
Photocopiable page, 'Five Old Fishermen'
Photocopiable page, 'Five Old Fishermen – poem frame' (versions 1 and 2)
Phase 3 activities
Photocopiable page, 'Rhyming couplets'
Phase 4 activities
Interactive activity, 'Finding rhymes' (versions 1 and 2)
Periodic assessment
Photocopiable page, 'Poetry 2 Reading assessment text'
Photocopiable page, 'Poetry 2 Reading assessment'
Recommended texts *The Smartest Giant in Town* (ISBN 978-0333963968); *Room on the Broom* (ISBN 978-0333903384); *The Gruffalo* (ISBN 978-0333710937) by Julia Donaldson.

Unit 2 ☐ Pattern and rhyme

Learning outcomes	Assessment opportunity and evidence	Assessment focuses (AFs)	Success criteria
		Level 1	

Phase ① activity page 150

| **Five little speckled frogs** Children can recite rhymes with repeating and predictable patterns using actions. | • Whole-class and independent activity where children identify rhymes and repeated words. • Performance of the action rhyme. • Children's completed interactive activity and oral responses. | **Reading AF5** Comments on obvious features of language. | I can say and perform an action rhyme. |

Phase ② activity page 151

| **Five old fishermen** Children can use rhymes as models for their own writing. | • Paired activity where children use a poem as a model to write their own version using a writing frame. • Discussion of the writing task. • Children's completed poems and oral evaluations. | **Writing AF7** • Mostly simple vocabulary. • Communicates meaning through repetition of key words. | I can use a frame for poetry writing. |

Phase ③ activity page 152

| **Rhyming stories** • Children can respond to simple patterned stories, identifying the patterned forms and use of rhyme. • Children can create their own rhyming couplets using playful language choices. | • Paired activity where children write their own rhyming couplets about a bird, using the photocopiable page for support. • Discussion of the task. • Children's completed photocopiable page and oral responses. | **Writing AF7** • Mostly simple vocabulary. • Communicates meaning through repetition of key words. | • I can respond to patterned stories. • I can create rhyming couplets. |

Phase ④ activity page 153

| **Finding rhymes** • Children can respond to a story written in rhyme. • Children can develop their vocabulary using rhyming dictionaries. | • Independent activity where children match a selection of rhyming words and add words orally from their own knowledge. • Children's completed interactive activity and oral responses. | **Reading AF1** • Some high frequency and familiar words read fluently and automatically. • Decode familiar and some unfamiliar words using blending as the prime approach. • Some awareness of punctuation marks. | • I can find words that rhyme. • I can use a rhyming dictionary to learn new words. |

Unit 2 ▢ Pattern and rhyme

Learning outcomes	Assessment opportunity and evidence	Assessment focuses (AFs)		Success criteria
		Level 2	Level 3	
Phase ① activity page 150				
Five little speckled frogs Children can recite rhymes with repeating and predictable patterns using actions.	● Whole-class and independent activity where children identify rhymes and repeated words. ● Performance of the action rhyme. ● Children's completed interactive activity and oral responses.	**Reading AF5** ● Some effective language choices noted. ● Some familiar patterns of language identified.	**Reading AF5** A few basic features of writer's use of language identified, but with little or no comment.	I can say and perform an action rhyme.
Phase ② activity page 151				
Five old fishermen Children can use rhymes as models for their own writing.	● Independent activity where children use a poem as a model to write their own version using a writing frame. ● Children's completed poems and oral evaluations.	**Writing AF7** ● Simple, often speech-like vocabulary conveys relevant meanings. ● Some adventurous word choices.	**Writing AF7** ● Simple, generally appropriate vocabulary used, limited in range. ● Some words selected for effect or occasion.	I can use a frame for poetry writing.
Phase ③ activity page 152				
Rhyming stories ● Children can respond to simple patterned stories, identifying the patterned forms and use of rhyme. ● Children can create their own rhyming couplets using playful language choices.	● Paired activity where children write their own rhyming couplets about a bird. ● Discussion of the task. ● Children's completed rhyming couplets and oral responses.	**Writing AF7** ● Simple, often speech-like vocabulary conveys relevant meanings. ● Some adventurous word choices.	**Writing AF7** ● Simple, generally appropriate vocabulary used, limited in range. ● Some words selected for effect or occasion.	● I can respond to patterned stories. ● I can create rhyming couplets.
Phase ③ activity page 153				
Finding rhymes ● Children can respond to a story written in rhyme. ● Children can develop their vocabulary using rhyming dictionaries.	● Independent activity where children match a selection of rhyming words and add words orally from their own knowledge. ● Children's completed interactive activity and oral responses.	**Reading AF1** ● Range of key words read on sight. ● Unfamiliar words decoded using appropriate strategies. ● Some fluency and expression.	**Reading AF1** Range of strategies used mostly effectively to read with fluency, understanding and expression.	● I can find words that rhyme. ● I can use a rhyming dictionary to learn new words.

Phase ① Five little speckled frogs

Learning outcome
Children can recite rhymes with repeating and predictable patterns using actions.

Success criteria
I can say and perform an action rhyme.

Setting the context
This assessment should be carried out once the children have listened to and joined in with rhymes and simple, patterned stories during shared and guided reading. They will have explored the different patterns created by the sounds, words and phrases and the way the text is laid out on the page or screen. They will also have investigated repeated patterns of particular words or phrases and rhyming words. Display the photocopiable page 'Five Little Speckled Frogs'. Read out the first verse and ask the children if any of them are familiar with it. Read the first verse again and encourage the children to join in with the remainder.

Assessment opportunity
Invite the children to complete the interactive activity 'Rhymes and patterns'. Afterwards, display the rhyme on the photocopiable page again and encourage the children to join in with actions. For example, clapping when words rhyme or stamping feet when words are repeated. Hold a plenary session and ask the children to say what they enjoy most about the poems they have been reading. Ask them to suggest how the poems would change if they did not use rhyme and repetition. Make notes of oral responses against the class list.

Assessment evidence
Oral responses from the children in the plenary might include 'They wouldn't be funny' or similar subjective responses. At level 3, the children might suggest that the poems would lose their rhythm. The completed interactive activity and oral responses will provide evidence against Reading AF5.

Next steps
Support: Work together to highlight the rhyming words in this and other poems.
Extension: Encourage the children to read other rhymes in groups and perform actions for the rhymes and/or repeated words.

Key aspects of learning
Enquiry: Children will hear, read and respond to rhymes and simple, patterned stories, exploring the patterns created by words and phrases.
Communication: Children will begin to develop their ability to discuss the language of poetry and to communicate through carefully chosen words. They will sometimes work collaboratively in pairs and groups. They will communicate outcomes orally, and in writing (possibly including ICT).

Phase ② Five old fishermen

Learning outcome
Children can use rhymes as models for their own writing.

Success criteria
I can use a frame for poetry writing.

Setting the context
Prior to this assessment, the children should have had the opportunity to write verses that: use patterned forms; play with words; rhyme and/or have repeated patterns. They should also have used simple writing frames in shared and guided writing. Display the photocopiable page 'Five Old Fishermen' and read the poem. Discuss the pattern and rhyme, and point out the humour in the last line. Explain to the children that they are going to write their own poems using this as a model.

Assessment opportunity
Provide the children with a copy of the photocopiable page 'Five Old Fishermen – poem frame' (version 1 for those at level 1; version 2 for those at levels 2–3). Ask them to fill in the blanks to create their own version of the poem. At level 1, the children can work with a partner. Afterwards, hold a plenary session and invite the children to read their poems aloud and give feedback on each other's work. Ask them to suggest which of the poems feature the most interesting images. Make notes of oral responses against the class list.

Assessment evidence
At level 1, the children will add simple words to the end of each line. At levels 2–3, the children may make more adventurous choices, adding new verbs and nouns to each line. The completed photocopiable pages and children's oral responses will provide evidence against Writing AF7.

Next steps
Support: Provide the children with a set of word cards featuring different nouns. Let them choose words to end each line of the poem to try out different effects.
Extension: Invite the children to write the poem again and change 'fishermen' to something new. For example, 'sailors' or 'pirates'.

Key aspects of learning
Enquiry: Children will hear, read and respond to rhymes and simple, patterned stories, exploring the patterns created by words and phrases.
Reasoning: Children will explain the words they and others chose to complete their compositions.
Empathy and self-awareness: Children will hear the patterns created by others and discuss their views – giving positive and constructive feedback.
Communication: Children will begin to develop their ability to discuss the language of poetry and to communicate through carefully chosen words. They will sometimes work collaboratively in pairs and groups. They will communicate outcomes orally, and in writing (possibly including ICT).

POETRY

Phase ③ Rhyming stories

Learning outcomes
● Children can respond to simple patterned stories, identifying the patterned forms and use of rhyme.
● Children can create their own rhyming couplets using playful language choices.

Success criteria
● I can respond to patterned stories.
● I can create rhyming couplets.

Setting the context
Perform this assessment once the children have listened to, read and responded to a variety of patterned stories. Examples might include *The Smartest Giant in Town*, *Room on the Broom* and *The Gruffalo* by Julia Donaldson. They should also have explored writing in different patterned forms during modelled, shared and guided writing sessions. For example, making up couplets based on rhyme and using playful language choices. Explain to the children that they are going to work in pairs to create their own rhyming couplets about a bird. Model creating an example such as:
A little brown sparrow flew to a tree
And in the branches, bumped into a bee.

Assessment opportunity
Provide the children with the photocopiable page 'Rhyming couplets' and invite them to experiment with adding words to the two lines to write their own rhyming couplet. The children working at level 3 can work without the photocopiable page. When the children have completed their couplets, collect them together and discuss the order in which they should be sequenced to create an extended poem. Read the couplets together and invite the children to say which ones use the most effective rhymes.

Assessment evidence
At level 1, the children will use rhymes and other words taken from the wordbank. At levels 2–3, the children will use words from their own knowledge. Use the children's completed couplets and oral contributions in the plenary to provide evidence against Writing AF7.

Next steps
Support: Provide the children with rhyming dictionaries to help them build their knowledge of rhyming words.
Extension: Encourage the children to add two more couplets to their original ones.

Key aspects of learning
Enquiry: Children will hear, read and respond to rhymes and simple, patterned stories, exploring the patterns created by words and phrases.
Reasoning: Children will explain the words they and others chose to complete their compositions.
Empathy and self-awareness: Children will hear the patterns created by others and discuss their views – giving positive and constructive feedback.
Communication: Children will begin to develop their ability to discuss the language of poetry and to communicate through carefully chosen words. They will sometimes work collaboratively in pairs and groups. They will communicate outcomes orally, and in writing (possibly including ICT).

Phase ④ Finding rhymes

Learning outcomes
- Children can respond to a story written in rhyme.
- Children can develop their vocabulary using rhyming dictionaries.

Success criteria
- I can find words that rhyme.
- I can use a rhyming dictionary to learn new words.

Setting the context
Prior to this assessment, the children should have had an opportunity to hear and read rhyming stories, and used these as models for their own writing. They should also have used rhyming dictionaries to extend their vocabulary. Invite the children working at level 1 to do version 1 of the interactive activity 'Finding rhymes'. The children working at levels 2–3 can complete version 2.

Assessment opportunity
Invite the children to read aloud their lists of words once they have dragged them to the correct space. Encourage them to say any other words that they can think of which would also rhyme. Make notes of the children's responses against the class list. Afterwards, discuss the activity with the children as part of a plenary session. Ask them to talk about the words that they found the hardest to match and why.

Assessment evidence
At level 1, the children will have some knowledge of simple, one-syllable rhyming words. At levels 2–3, the children will recognise words of more than one syllable and different spelling patterns that rhyme. Use the completed interactive activities and the children's oral responses to provide evidence against Reading AF1.

Next steps
Support: Encourage the children to use rhyming dictionaries when writing poems, to build up their store of rhyming words.
Extension: Encourage the children to create their own rhyming wordbanks.

Key aspects of learning
Enquiry: Children will hear, read and respond to rhymes and simple, patterned stories, exploring the patterns created by words and phrases.
Communication: Children will begin to develop their ability to discuss the language of poetry and to communicate through carefully chosen words. They will sometimes work collaboratively in pairs and groups. They will communicate outcomes orally, and in writing (possibly including ICT).

Periodic assessment

Reading

Learning outcomes
- Children can respond to simple patterned stories, identifying the patterned forms and use of rhymes.
- Children can hear, read and respond to story written in rhyme.

Success criteria
- I can explore how rhymes are created by the way the text is laid out on the page.
- I can hear, read and respond to a simple, patterned story.

Setting the context
Review the poetry that you have read during the course of this unit. Ask the children to comment on the poems, stating which poems they preferred and giving their reasons why. Display the photocopiable page 'Poetry 2 Reading assessment text' and read the simple, patterned story 'The Mouse, the Frog and the Little Red Hen' through together. Invite the children to identify the rhyming words and repeated phrases by underlining or highlighting them on screen or on their own copies. Make notes of their responses against the class list.

Assessment opportunity
Arrange the children into groups of three or four and invite them to complete the sequencing activity on the photocopiable page 'Poetry 2 Reading assessment'. Explain that they should cut out all the lines from the story in the table, divide them among the group and collaborate to work out how to sequence the story. Invite the groups to read their completed sequence aloud and compare how the groups have ordered the lines.

Assessment evidence
At level 1, the children should recognise simple repetitions in the text. For example, 'frog', 'hen' and 'mouse', and the repeated phrases, 'Not I' and 'Who'll'. At levels 2-3, the children may recognise the words the hen says that are a repetition of the same meaning. For example, 'Red Hen made no reply' and 'Little Red Hen said never a word'. Use this activity and the children's oral responses to provide evidence against Reading AF5.

Periodic assessment

Writing

Learning outcome
Children can use rhymes and stories as models for their own writing.

Success criteria
I can use a simple model from reading as a frame for writing.

Setting the context
Collect the work that has been completed during the course of this unit and discuss achievements with the children, individually.

Assessment opportunity
Ask the children to look back at their 'Five Old Fishermen' poems (written in phase 2) and evaluate how they could be improved based on what they have learned. Make notes of their responses against the class list.

Assessment evidence
At level 1, the children might comment on the layout and presentation rather than content. At levels 2-3, the children will begin to think more critically about their word choices and suggest better alternatives. Use the children's completed photocopiable pages and work done throughout the unit to provide evidence against Writing AF1.

POETRY

Five Old Fishermen

Five old fishermen
sitting on a bridge
One caught a tiddler
One caught a fridge

One caught a tadpole
One caught an eel
And the fifth one caught
a perambulator wheel.

Anon

Illustration © 2010, Anna Godwin/The Illustrator Agency.

Name   Date

POETRY

Five Old Fishermen – poem frame (1)

◢ Write a new version of the poem, 'Five Old Fishermen'.

Five old fishermen

sitting on a _____

One caught a _____

One caught a _____

One caught a _____

One caught a _____

And the fifth one caught _____ .

Red
Amber   I can use a frame for poetry writing. ☐
Green

Illustration © 2010, Anna Godwin/The Illustrator Agency.

Name   Date

Rhyming couplets

◾ Add your own words to write a rhyming couplet. Use some of the words from the wordbank to help you think of ideas.

A little brown sparrow _____

_____

And in the _____

_____

Rhyming words:

tree	sky	moon	house	log
flea	fly	spoon	mouse	frog
donkey	spy	balloon	louse	dog

Red
Amber
Green

I can create rhyming couplets. ⬜

Illustration © 2010, Anna Godwin/The Illustrator Agency.

Poetry 2 Reading assessment

■ Cut out all the sentences. Share them around the group and work out how to sequence them to tell the story.

✂

Once a Mouse, a Frog and a Little Red Hen,	The work all fell on the Little Red Hen,	And away with the loaf she flew.
Said the lazy Mouse, 'Not I.'	And lazier still was the Mouse.	And sometimes hunt the food.
But flew around with bowl and spoon,	'Nor I,' croaked the Frog as he drowsed in the shade,	Together kept a house;
And while the bread was baking brown,	'Who'll set the table?' she said.	Red Hen made no reply,
Said she, 'Now who will make some bread?'	And build the fires, and scrub, and cook,	And mixed and stirred the rye.
'Who'll make the fire to bake the bread?'	'Not I,' said the sleepy Frog with a yawn;	'Oh, no, you won't!' said the Little Red Hen,
Who had to get the wood,	She found a bag of rye;	Said the Mouse again, 'Not I,'
'Nor I,' said the Mouse again.	But a roaring fire she made;	'I will!' cried the Frog. 'And I!' squeaked the Mouse,
One day, as she went scratching round,	The Frog was the laziest of frogs,	And, scarcely opening his sleepy eyes,
As they near the table drew;	So the table she set and the bread put on,	'Who'll eat this bread?' said the Hen.
The Little Red Hen said never a word,	Frog made the same reply.	**The Mouse, the Frog and the Little Red Hen**

POETRY
UNIT 3 Poems on a theme

Literacy objectives

Speak and listen for a wide range of purposes in different contexts

Strand 1 Speaking
- Interpret a text by reading aloud with some variety of pace and emphasis.

Strand 2 Listening and responding
- Listen with sustained concentration, building new stores of words in different contexts.

Strand 3 Group discussion and interaction
- Ask and answer questions, make relevant contributions, offer suggestions and take turns.

Read and write for a range of purposes on paper and on screen

Strand 5 Word recognition: decoding (reading) and encoding (spelling)
- Recognise and use alternative ways of pronouncing the graphemes already taught.
- Recognise and use alternative ways of spelling the phonemes already taught.
- Identify the constituent parts of two-syllable and three-syllable words to support the application of phonic knowledge and skills.
- Recognise automatically an increasing number of familiar high frequency words.
- Apply phonic knowledge and skills as the prime approach to reading and spelling unfamiliar words that are not completely decodable.
- Read more challenging texts which can be decoded using their acquired phonic knowledge and skills, along with automatic recognition of high frequency words.
- Read and spell phonically decodable two-syllable and three-syllable words.

Strand 6 Word structure and spelling
- Spell new words using phonics as the prime approach.
- Segment sounds into their constituent phonemes in order to spell them correctly.
- Recognise and use alternative ways of spelling the graphemes already taught.
- Use knowledge of common inflections in spelling, such as plurals, -*ly*, -*er*.
- Read and spell phonically decodable two-syllable and three-syllable words.

Strand 7 Understanding and interpreting texts
- Explore the effect of patterns of language and repeated words and phrases.

Strand 8 Engaging with and responding to texts
- Visualise and comment on events, characters and ideas, making imaginative links to their own experiences.

Strand 9 Creating and shaping texts
- Find and use new and interesting words and phrases, including story language.
- Create short simple texts on paper and screen that combine words with images (and sounds).

Key aspects of learning

Enquiry
- Children will listen to poems on a theme and consider how they feel about the subject.

Reasoning
- Children will explain their preferences for different poems. They will explain the words and phrases they chose to describe different aspects of the theme.

Key aspects of learning (continued)

Evaluation
● Children will discuss success criteria, give feedback to others and judge the effectiveness of their own word choices.

Empathy and self-awareness
● Children will read and hear about the experiences of others and compare it to their own.

Communication
● Children will begin to develop their ability to discuss the language of poetry and to communicate their own experiences and observations through carefully chosen words. They will sometimes work collaboratively in pairs and groups. They will communicate outcomes orally, and in writing (possibly including ICT).

Assessment focuses

Reading

AF2 *(understand, describe, select or retrieve information, events or ideas from texts and use quotation and reference to text).*
AF5 *(explain and comment on writers' use of language, including grammatical and literary features at word and sentence level).*
AF6 *(identify and comment on writers' purposes and viewpoints, and the overall effect of the text on the reader).*

Writing

AF7 *(select appropriate and effective vocabulary).*

Speaking and listening

Speaking (speak with clarity, intonation and pace).
Listening and responding (listen with sustained concentration).
Group discussion and interaction (listen to each other's views and preferences).

Resources

Phase 1 activities
Photocopiable page, 'Moving Away'
Photocopiable page, 'My Friend'
Photocopiable page, 'Last Lick'
Photocopiable page, 'Friends' (versions 1 and 2)
Interactive activity, 'Powerful words'
Phase 2 activities
Photocopiable page, 'Lion'
Photocopiable page, 'Word tiles'
Photocopiable page, 'In my box'
Phase 3 activities
Photocopiable page, 'The Really Rocking Rocket Trip'
Interactive activity, 'Performance poetry'
Periodic assessment
Interactive activity, 'Poetry 3 Reading assessment'
Photocopiable page, 'Poetry 3 Writing assessment'
Recommended texts
'The Magic Box' by Kit Wright (ISBN 978-0230-70515-9)
'Secret Poem' by Pie Corbett, from *The Works 4* (ISBN 978-0330-43644-1)
'A Feather from an Angel' by Brian Moses (visit www.poetryzone.ndirect.co.uk)

Unit 3 📖 Poems on a theme

Learning outcomes	Assessment opportunity and evidence	Assessment focuses (AFs)	Success criteria
		Level 1	
Phase ① activities pages 165-166			
Poems on a theme Children can listen to and respond to poems on a theme.	• Paired and supported group activity where children compare three poems on a similar theme. • Discussion of the poems, identifying similarities and differences. • Children's completed photocopiable page and oral responses.	**Reading AF2** • Some simple points from familiar texts recalled. • Some pages/sections of interest located. **Reading AF6** Some simple comments about preferences, mostly linked to own experience.	I can listen to and respond to poems on a theme.
Powerful words and phrases Children can suggest powerful words linked to the theme.	• Independent activity where children choose from a selection of powerful words to complete a poem. • Children's completed interactive activity and oral responses.	**Writing AF7** • Mostly simple vocabulary. • Communicates meaning through repetition of key words.	I can make word collections based on my own experiences and feelings.
Phase ② activities pages 166-167			
Creating free verse Children can create a powerful phrase using carefully chosen vocabulary to contribute to a class free verse.	• Small group activity where children create a group poem by choosing words and sticking them onto a poetry frame. Groups then perform their poems and the audience give feedback. • Discussion of the task and planning of the oral performance. • Children's completed poems and group evaluations.	**Writing AF7** • Mostly simple vocabulary. • Communicates meaning through repetition of key words.	• I can use free verse. • I can notice patterns in a poem and use them as a model for my own writing.
Phase ③ activities pages 167-168			
Performing a poem Children can perform a poem and identify the criteria for a successful performance.	• Supported small group activity where children perform a given poem. • Discussion of the task, planning and rehearsing the poetry performance. • Children's completed interactive activity, group performance and oral responses.	**Reading AF5** Comments on obvious features of language.	• I can perform a poem. • I can identify success criteria for a performance.
Phase ④ activity page 168			
Comparing poems Children can make comparisons between poems and give reasons for their opinions and preferences.	• Independent activity where children choose their favourite poem from those read in the unit, read it aloud and say why they chose it. • Children's oral responses.	**Reading AF5** Comments on obvious features of language.	• I can compare similarities and differences between poems. • I can talk about what I think about a poem and give reasons.

Unit 3 ▢ Poems on a theme

Learning outcomes	Assessment opportunity and evidence	Assessment focuses (AFs)		Success criteria
		Level 2	Level 3	
Phase ① activities pages 165-166				
Poems on a theme Children can listen to and respond to poems on a theme.	● Paired activity where children compare three poems on a similar theme. ● Discussion of the poems, identifying similarities and differences. ● Children's completed photocopiable page and oral responses.	**Reading AF2** ● Some specific, straightforward information recalled. ● Generally clear idea of where to look for information. **Reading AF6** ● Some awareness that writers have viewpoints and purposes. ● Simple statements about likes and dislikes in reading, sometimes with reasons.	**Reading AF2** ● Simple, most obvious points identified though there may also be some misunderstanding. ● Some comments include quotations from or references to text, but not always relevant. **Reading AF6** ● Comments identify main purpose. ● Express personal response but with little awareness of writer's viewpoint or effect on reader.	I can listen to and respond to poems on a theme.
Powerful words and phrases Children can suggest powerful words linked to the theme.	● Independent activity where children choose from a selection of powerful words to complete a poem. ● Children's completed interactive activity and oral responses.	**Writing AF7** ● Simple, often speech-like vocabulary conveys relevant meanings. ● Some adventurous word choices.	**Writing AF7** ● Simple, generally appropriate vocabulary used, limited in range. ● Some words selected for effect or occasion.	I can make word collections based on my own experiences and feelings.
Phase ② activities pages 166-167				
Creating free verse Children can create a powerful phrase using carefully chosen vocabulary to contribute to a class free verse.	● Small group activity where children create a group poem by choosing words and sticking them onto a poetry frame. Groups then perform their poems and the audience give feedback. ● Discussion of the task and planning of the oral performance. ● Children's completed poems and group evaluations.	**Writing AF7** ● Simple, often speech-like vocabulary conveys relevant meanings. ● Some adventurous word choices.	**Writing AF7** ● Simple, generally appropriate vocabulary used, limited in range. ● Some words selected for effect or occasion.	● I can use free verse. ● I can notice patterns in a poem and use them as a model for my own writing.
Phase ③ activities pages 167-168				
Performing a poem Children can perform a poem and identify the criteria for a successful performance.	● Small group activity where children perform a given poem. ● Discussion of the task, planning and rehearsing the poetry performance. ● Children's completed interactive activity, group performance and oral responses.	**Reading AF5** ● Some effective language choices noted. ● Some familiar patterns of language identified.	**Reading AF5** A few basic features of writer's use of language identified, but with little or no comment.	● I can perform a poem. ● I can identify success criteria for a performance.

Unit 3 📖 Poems on a theme

Learning outcomes	Assessment opportunity and evidence	Assessment focuses (AFs)		Success criteria
		Level 2	Level 3	
Phase ④ activity page 168				
Comparing poems Children can make comparisons between poems and give reasons for their opinions and preferences.	● Independent activity where children choose their favourite poem from those read in the unit, read it aloud and say why they chose it. ● Children's oral responses.	**Reading AF5** ● Some effective language choices noted. ● Some familiar patterns of language identified.	**Reading AF5** A few basic features of writer's use of language identified, but with little or no comment.	● I can compare similarities and differences between poems. ● I can talk about what I think about a poem and give reasons.

📖SCHOLASTIC

Phase ① Poems on a theme

Learning outcome
Children can listen to poems and select their favourite parts.

Success criteria
I can listen to and respond to poems on a theme.

Setting the context
Prior to this assessment, the children should have listened to and responded to a variety of poems on a theme. They should have had the opportunity to discuss their responses to the poems, identify their favourite parts and explore similarities and differences. Display and read the three poems on the photocopiable pages ('Moving Away', 'My Friend' and 'Last Lick'). Invite the children to say what they think the theme is.

Assessment opportunity
In pairs, provide the children with copies of the photocopiable page 'Friends'. At level 1, the children should work in a group with a supporting adult, using version 1 of the photocopiable page. Read the questions from the photocopiable page and ask the pairs to discuss their opinions before writing them on the page. Encourage them to add any other details they notice about the poems, such as similarities and differences, the way they are laid out, use of language and patterns and so on. Hold a plenary session and ask the children to say what they enjoyed most about the poems. Make notes of oral responses against the class list.

Assessment evidence
At level 1, the children may need prompting to find and understand the overall theme of the three poems. At levels 2–3, the children may comment on differences between the poems. For example, "Moving Away' is a sad poem' and "Last Lick' is a happy poem'. Use the children's completed photocopiable pages and oral responses to provide evidence against Reading AF2 and AF6.

Next steps
Support: Encourage the children to read 'Last Lick' in guided reading and find all the rhyming words and present-tense verbs.
Extension: Encourage the children to read and compare other poems on the theme of friends.

Key aspects of learning
Enquiry: Children will listen to poems on a theme, compare them and consider how they feel about the poems.
Reasoning: Children will explain their preferences for different poems. They will explain the words and phrases they chose to describe different aspects of the theme.
Empathy and self-awareness: Children will read and hear about the experiences of others and compare it to their own.
Communication: Children will begin to develop their ability to discuss the language of poetry and to communicate their own experiences and observations through carefully chosen words. They will sometimes work collaboratively in pairs and groups. They will communicate outcomes orally, and in writing (possibly including ICT).

POETRY

Phase ① Powerful words and phrases

Learning outcome
Children can suggest powerful words linked to the theme.

Success criteria
I can make word collections based on my own experiences and feelings.

Setting the context
The children should have already had experience of identifying powerful words and phrases in poetry and used examples of these in shared and modelled writing sessions. Invite them to complete the interactive activity 'Powerful words'. On each screen, there is a series of sentences about a friend. The children must choose from a series of powerful words to complete each sentence.

Assessment opportunity
Hold a plenary session and invite the children to compare their choices and say why they chose them. Encourage the children to suggest other words they could have used for each of the sentences. Make notes of their responses against the class list.

Assessment evidence
At level 1, the children may justify their choices by suggesting the sound of the word suits the sentence. At levels 2-3, the children may demonstrate more adventurous choices orally. The completed interactive activity and children's oral responses will provide evidence against Writing AF7.

Next steps
Support: Identify powerful words and phrases in other friend-themed poems.
Extension: Invite the children to write out the sentences from the interactive activity and add their own powerful words.

Key aspects of learning
Reasoning: Children will explain their preferences for different poems. They will explain the words and phrases they chose to describe different aspects of the theme.
Evaluation: Children will discuss success criteria, give feedback to others and judge the effectiveness of their own word choices.
Communication: Children will begin to develop their ability to discuss the language of poetry and to communicate their own experiences and observations through carefully chosen words. They will sometimes work collaboratively in pairs and groups. They will communicate outcomes orally, and in writing (possibly including ICT).

Phase ② Creating free verse

Learning outcome
Children can create a powerful phrase using carefully chosen vocabulary to contribute to a class free verse.

Success criteria
● I can use free verse.
● I can notice patterns in a poem and use them as a model for my own writing.

Setting the context
Prior to this assessment, the children should have already experienced writing a simple patterned poem on a theme, and explored imaginative and fanciful poems such as 'The Magic Box' by Kit Wright, 'Secret Poem' by Pie Corbett and 'A Feather from an Angel' by Brian Moses. Display the photocopiable page 'Lion' and read the poem together. Ask the children to identify the verses and find the rhymes. Encourage them to find the words used to describe the lion.

Assessment opportunity

Arrange the children into small groups. Provide them with the word tiles from the photocopiable page 'Word tiles'. Ask the groups to choose words from their selection to stick onto the spaces on the photocopiable page 'In my box', to create a group poem. At level 1, the children can work together to create one verse. At levels 2-3, the children can create a verse each. Invite the groups to read their poems aloud. Discuss their word choices and how they were combined. Encourage them to evaluate other groups' poems by highlighting any unusual combinations of words.

Assessment evidence

At level 1, the children will tend to put words together conventionally to describe appearance. At levels 2-3, the children will start to use more imaginative combinations of words to describe movement and appearance. Use the children's completed poems and oral contributions to provide evidence against Writing AF7.

Next steps

Support: Find unusual images in poetry during guided reading sessions.
Extension: Ask the children to each add another verse to their group poem.

Key aspects of learning

Reasoning: Children will explain their preferences for different poems. They will explain the words and phrases they chose to describe different aspects of the theme.
Evaluation: Children will discuss success criteria, give feedback to others and judge the effectiveness of their own word choices.
Communication: Children will begin to develop their ability to discuss the language of poetry and to communicate their own experiences and observations through carefully chosen words. They will sometimes work collaboratively in pairs and groups. They will communicate outcomes orally, and in writing (possibly including ICT).

Phase ③ Performing a poem

Learning outcome
Children can perform a poem and identify the criteria for a successful performance.

Success criteria
● I can perform a poem.
● I can identify success criteria for a performance.

Setting the context

The children should have explored different ways of performing a poem using actions, props, music and dance, written a collaborative poem in groups or as a whole class and worked out a group performance. Divide the class into small groups. Give each group a copy of the photocopiable page 'The Really Rocking Rocket Trip'. Read the poem to the class and then read it through a second time together.

Assessment opportunity

Invite the groups to complete the interactive activity 'Performance poetry'. This will highlight the features in the poem that will help them to perform it. Allow the children time to discuss their approach to the performance, gather props and rehearse. Remind the class about the agreed success criteria for performing a poem. Invite the groups to perform their poems. When all groups have performed, encourage the class to give feedback about the poem and performance. Note strong use of rhythm in a performance. Make notes against the class list.

Assessment evidence

At level 1, the children are likely to need adult support to help them identify the language features of the poem. At levels 2-3, the children will identify correctly some of the language features of the poem but their comments on the effect of these features will be very limited. Use the completed interactive activity and oral feedback to provide evidence against Reading AF5.

Next steps
Support: To practice performing, ask children to read small sections of a poem aloud.
Extension: Encourage the children to perform their poem to another class.

Key aspects of learning
Enquiry: Children will listen to poems and explore props and actions to help them perform.
Evaluation: Children will discuss success criteria, give feedback to others and judge the effectiveness of their own word choices.
Communication: Children will begin to develop their ability to discuss the language of poetry and to communicate their own experiences and observations through carefully chosen words. They will sometimes work collaboratively in pairs and groups. They will communicate outcomes orally, and in writing (possibly including ICT).

Phase ④ Comparing poems

Learning outcome
Children can make comparisons between poems and give reasons for their opinions and preferences.

Success criteria
● I can compare similarities and differences between poems.
● I can talk about what I think about a poem and give reasons.

Setting the context
The children should have had the opportunity to write their own simple, patterned texts on a given theme, shared and discussed their outcomes and evaluated them against agreed success criteria. Ask the children to choose their favourite poem from this unit, read it aloud to others in their group or class and tell the audience why they chose this particular poem. Invite them to say which poem had the best pattern to use as a starting point for writing their own versions and give a reason for their choice. Make notes of their responses against the class list.

Assessment opportunity
This activity provides an opportunity to assess the children's ability to read and compare poems on a theme and express their opinions. It also allows you to assess how well the children responded to writing poems based on a pattern from reading.

Assessment evidence
At level 1, the children may give simple reasons for their choices such as 'I liked the way it rhymed'. At levels 2–3, the children may refer to the strong rhythm and/or the poet's use of powerful words. Use the children's oral responses to provide evidence against Reading AF5.

Next steps
Support: During guided reading, invite the children to express their opinions about the author's choices of words, in both poetry and stories.
Extension: Encourage the children to take favourite poems home to read to a parent or grandparent.

Key aspects of learning
Enquiry: Children will listen to poems on a theme and consider how they feel about the subject.
Evaluation: Children will discuss success criteria, give feedback to others and judge the effectiveness of their own word choices.
Communication: Children will begin to develop their ability to discuss the language of poetry and to communicate their own experiences and observations through carefully chosen words. They will sometimes work collaboratively in pairs and groups. They will communicate outcomes orally, and in writing (possibly including ICT).

Periodic assessment

Reading

Learning outcome Children can identify poetic features and patterns in poems on a common theme.	**Success criteria** I can identify patterns, rhyme and powerful words in poems. **Setting the context** Review the poetry that has been studied during the course of this unit. Ask the children to tell you which of the poems they felt had the strongest patterned language, which used the most powerful words and which made the best use of rhyme. Remind the children of the other types of poetry read in the previous units. Encourage them to discuss how they were similar or different and identify any common features. Encourage them to describe how the poems made them feel when they first read particular ones. **Assessment opportunity** Support the children working at level 1 to deepen their responses by asking questions such as *Which poem most appealed to your feelings? Did some poems make you look differently at something?* Invite the children to complete the interactive activity 'Poetry 3 Reading assessment'. They will be asked to agree or disagree with a series of simple statements about the poetry that they have read over the course of the unit. **Assessment evidence** At level 1, the children will show an awareness of rhyme, rhythm and repetition. At level 3, the children will start to demonstrate an awareness that poetic form can be varied and that words are carefully chosen to create images and feelings. Use the interactive activity, the children's oral responses and evidence gathered throughout this unit to provide evidence against Reading AF4 and AF5.

Writing

Learning outcome Children can select their favourite poems and give reasons for their choices.	**Success criteria** • I can use free verse. • I can notice patterns in a poem and use them as a model for my own writing. • I can express my opinions about a poem. **Setting the context** Collect the work that has been completed during the course of this unit and discuss the children's achievements with them, individually. Ask them to say which poetry writing they found the most enjoyable. **Assessment opportunity** Invite the children to choose their favourite piece of written work from the unit and, using the photocopiable page 'Poetry 3 Writing assessment', ask them to write a review of the features of the poem for a class display. **Assessment evidence** At level 1, the children should be able to say what their poem is about, their favourite words and how the poem makes them feel. At levels 2-3, the children will be able to suggest an audience for their poem. Use the children's completed photocopiable pages and work completed throughout the unit to provide evidence against Writing AF2.

POETRY

Moving Away

My best friend's leaving school today,
she's moving somewhere new.
Her house is on the market,
her brother's going too…

I saw the lorry loading
   her toys
   her coat
   her hat…
   her bike
   and books
   and bedclothes
   her hamster and her cat.

She said –
   she'd come and see me,

I said –
   I'd go and see her,
but I don't like these changes
   I liked things as they were.

Peter Dixon

Text © 2001, Peter Dixon. Illustration © 2010, Anna Godwin/The Illustrator Agency.

POETRY

My Friend

my friend is
like bark
rounding a tree

he warms
like sun
on a winter day

he cools
like water
in the hot noon

his voice
is ready
as a spring bird

he is
my friend
and I
am his

Emily Hearn

POETRY

Name _____   Date _____

Friends (1)

◼ Write about the poems with a partner.

1. What are the three poems about?

_____

_____

_____

2. Find two rhymes in the poem 'Moving Away'.

_____

_____

3. In 'My Friend', what does the poet say the friend is like?

_____

_____

4. Which poem do you like best?

_____

5. What is your favourite part?

_____

_____

Red ⃝
Amber ⃝
Green ⃝

PHOTOCOPIABLE **◼SCHOLASTIC**

Name _____ Date _____

In my box

- Stick word tiles onto the spaces to make a group poem.

I have a box in which I keep a			
My			
And		
My			

I can use free verse. ☐

I can notice patterns in a poem and use them as a model for my own writing. ☐

Red
Amber
Green

⬤⬤⬤

 Transitional assessment

Activity	Type	Level	Description
1.1	Reading comprehension	1	No time limit; two-part test based on non-fiction information text about animals and a narrative extract from *Duck in the Truck* by Jez Alborough
1.1	Shorter writing task	1	15 minutes; writing a recount about a favourite place you have visited
1.1	Longer writing task	1	25 minutes; writing a story about five little ducks that become lost (based on the traditional rhyme 'Five Little Ducks')
2.1	Reading comprehension	2	30-minute two-part test based on a narrative extract from *The Snow Lambs* by Debbie Gliori and the poem 'Weather at Work' by Jenny Morris
2.1	Shorter writing task	2	15 minutes; writing a report about different kinds of weather
2.1	Longer writing task	2	30 minutes; writing a recount based on personal experience of problem weather
3.1	Reading comprehension	3	30-minute two-part test based on narrative extracts from *The Sheep Pig* by Dick King-Smith and a non-fiction leaflet for a farm visitors' centre
3.1	Shorter writing task	3	15 minutes; writing an imaginative description of a special pet
3.1	Longer writing task	3	30 minutes; writing letter to persuade the teacher to take the class on a trip to a farm

NB There are two transitional assessments provided for each level. Transitional tests and tasks 1.2, 2.2 and 3.2 are not shown here. All tests and tasks are available on the CD-ROM.

Reading tests: instructions

There are two reading comprehension tests provided at each level (levels 1-3) on the CD-ROM. Each reading test is divided into two parts.

Administering the test
- There is no time limit for both parts of the test at level 1.
  - Photocopy the two short texts for each child.
  - Children should read aloud the texts with adult support only given when a child has clearly used all the reading strategies that they know.
  - After their reading of a text, ask the child the appropriate questions.
  - Children should answer questions orally.
- Allow 30 minutes for both parts of the test at levels 2 and 3.
  - Children should work unaided: do not read questions or words to them.

Equipment for each child:
- Pencil, eraser (or children may cross out mistakes).

Marking and levelling the children
- Mark the test using the Reading Mark Scheme provided on CD-ROM.
- Add together the marks from both parts of the reading tests (possible total of 30 marks).
- Use the levelling grid at the end of the Mark Scheme to level the test.
- When awarding an end-of-year Teacher Assessment Level, you will need to consider a child's performance during Periodic and Day-to-Day Assessments. If a child has achieved level 3 or above in the transitional tests, it can be assumed that they have achieved AF1 at that level.

Writing tasks: instructions

There are two writing tasks provided at each level (levels 1-3) on the CD-ROM. Each writing task is divided into two parts: shorter and longer writing tasks.

Administering the tasks
Shorter writing task
Allow 15 minutes for each task at level 1, and 20 minutes at levels 2 and 3.
Longer writing task
Allow 25 minutes for each task at level 1, and 30 minutes at levels 2 and 3.
- Children should sit so that they cannot see each other's work.
- Read the task to the children; do not explain the task or help them.
- The task may be administered to groups of children or to the whole class.
- Do not allow children to use dictionaries or word books.

Equipment for each child:
Pencil, eraser (or children may cross out mistakes) and sheets of plain paper.

Introducing the writing tasks
At level 1, each task should be introduced to the children following the task guidelines. At levels 2 and 3 say to the children: *I am going to ask you to do some writing. I will read the task to you, but I cannot help you with your ideas. If you make a mistake, cross it out (or rub it out neatly) and write your word clearly. Spell the words as best you can, building them up as you usually do.*

Marking and levelling the children
- Mark each piece of writing separately using the Writing Mark Scheme, Table 1, provided on the CD-ROM.
- Double the marks gained for the longer Writing task and add this total to the mark gained for the shorter Writing task.
- Assess spelling and handwriting across both pieces of writing using Table 2, provided on the CD-ROM.
- Add the total gained from Table 1 to the total from Table 2.
- Use the grid at the end of the Mark Scheme to find a level for each child.